Mindfulness Coloring Book for Teens and Adults

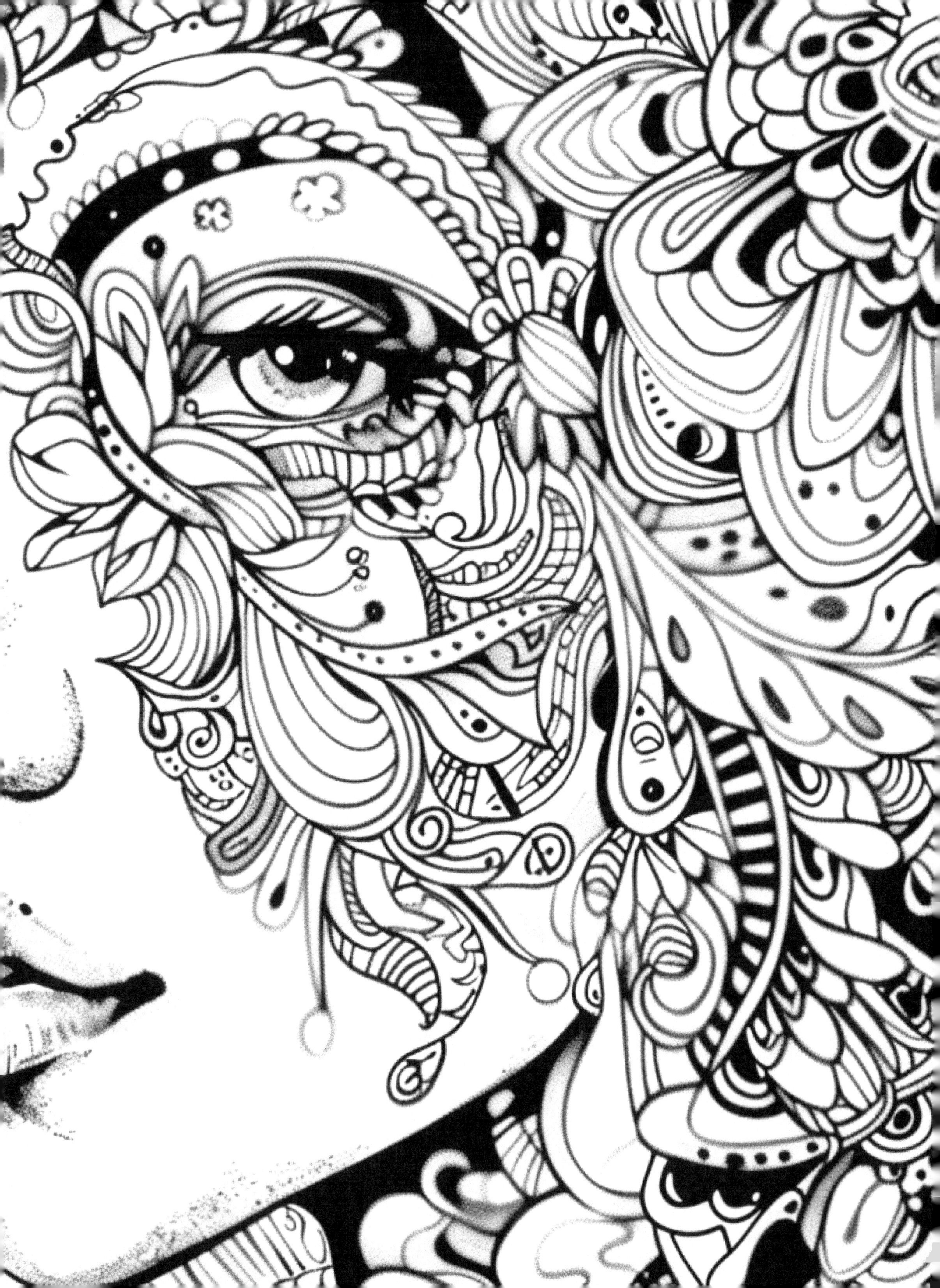

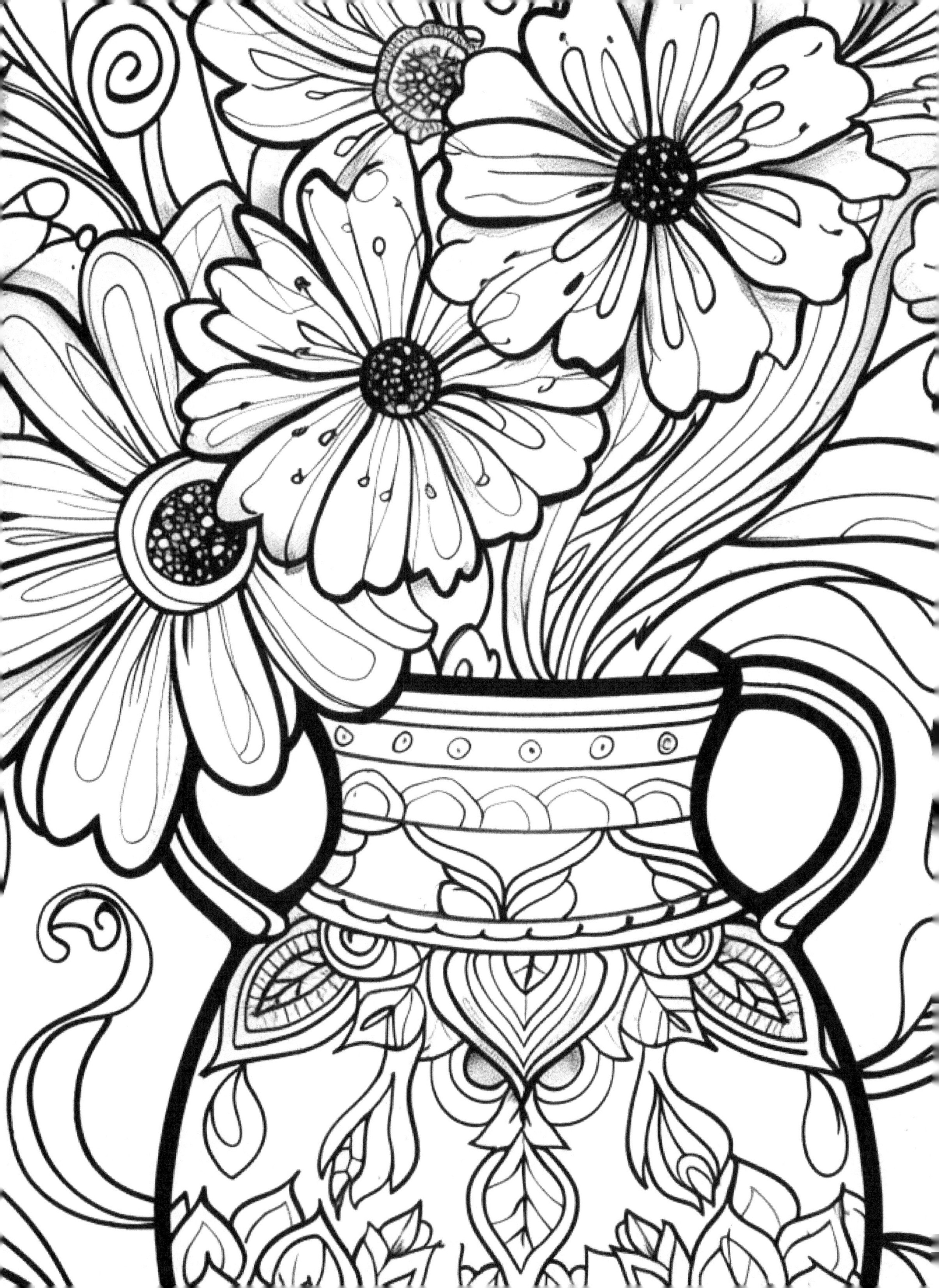

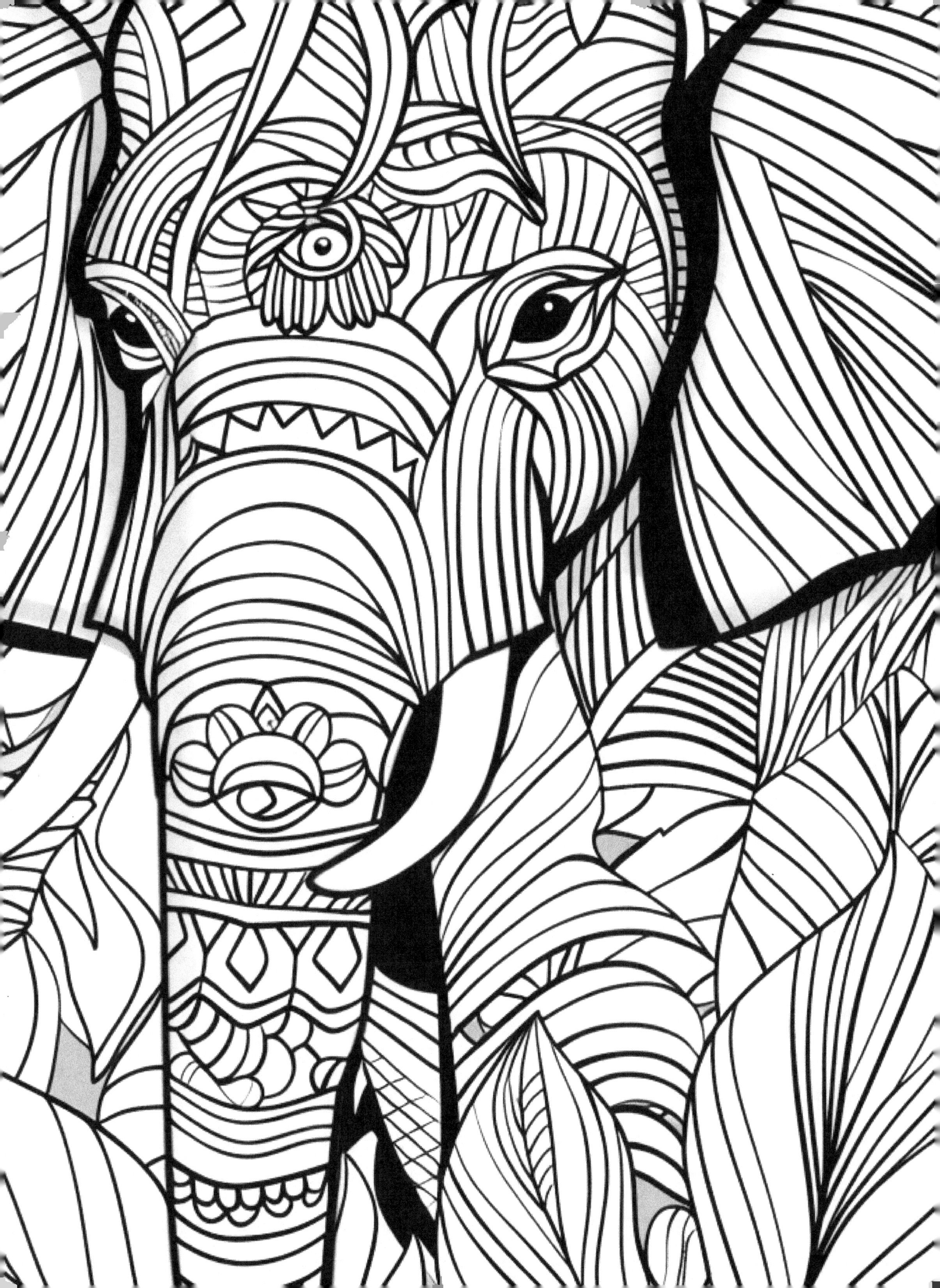

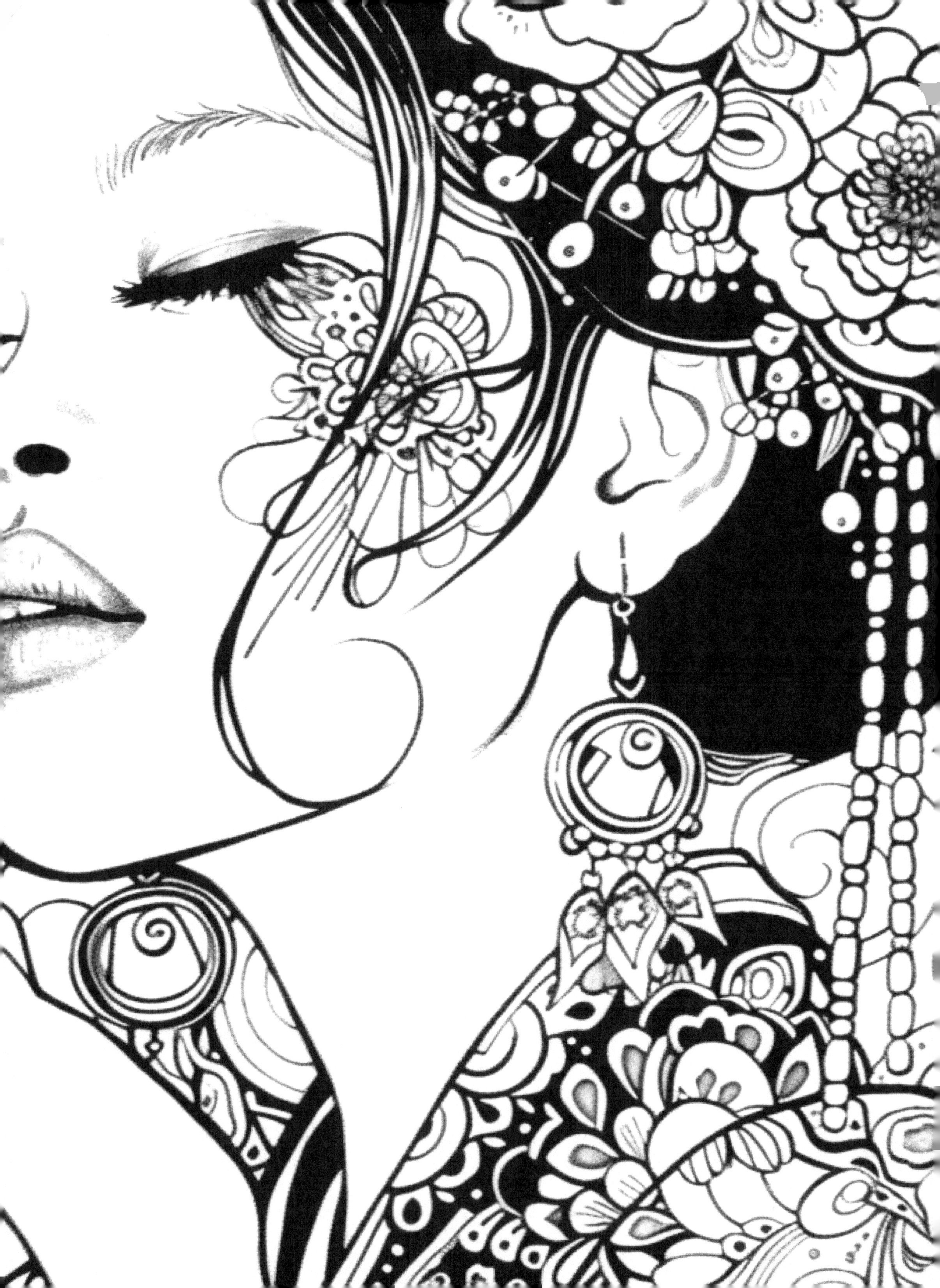

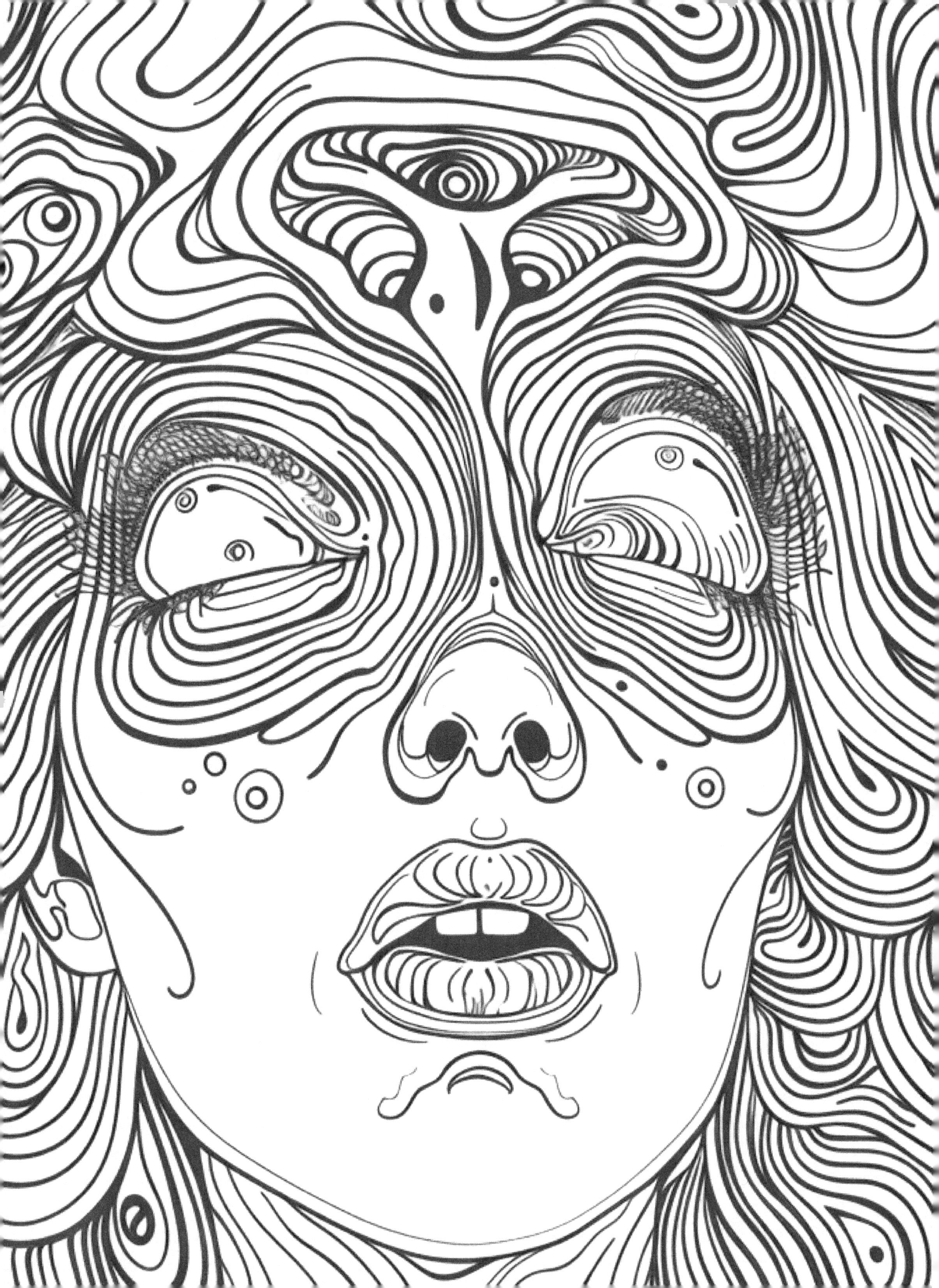

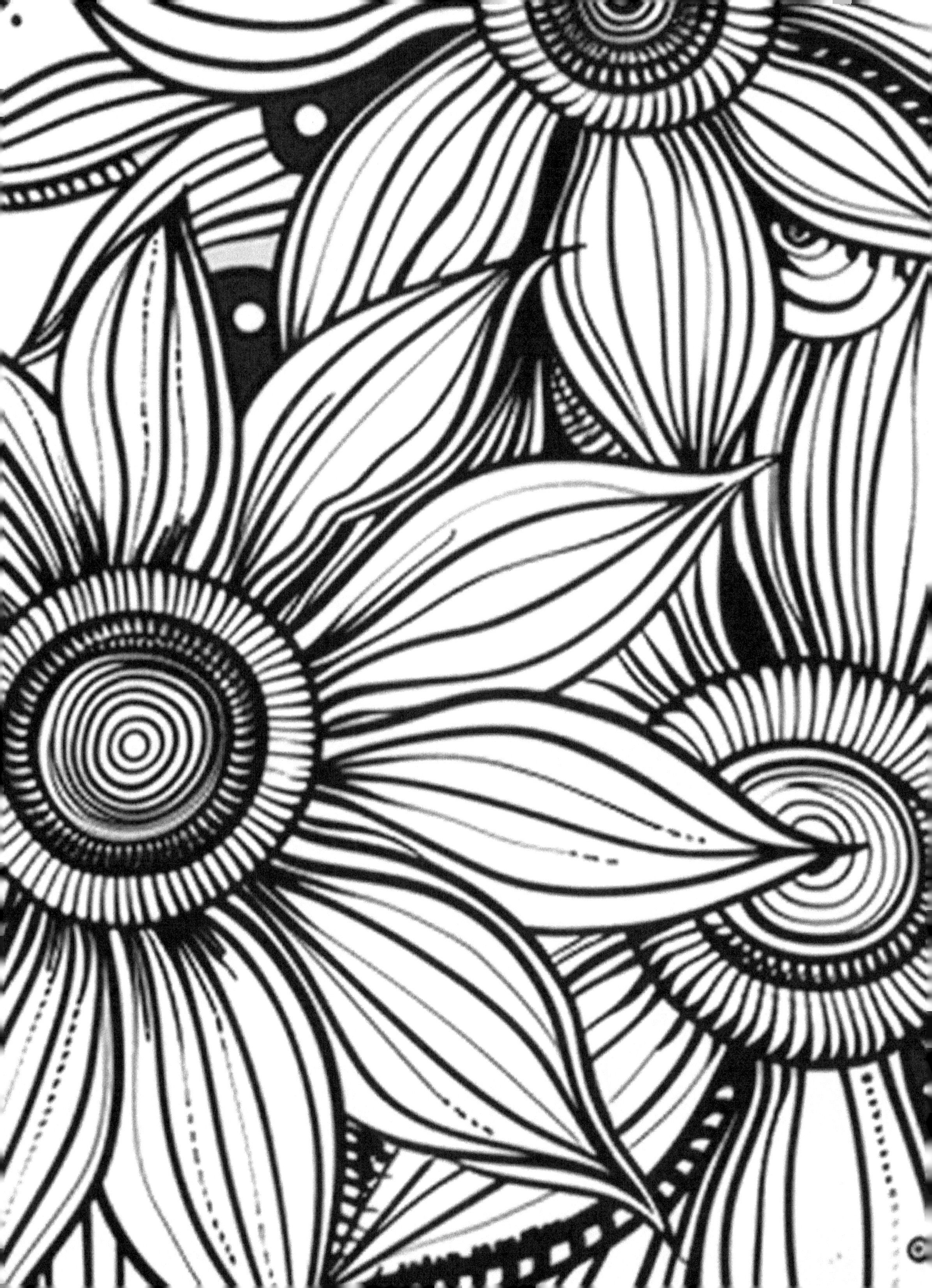

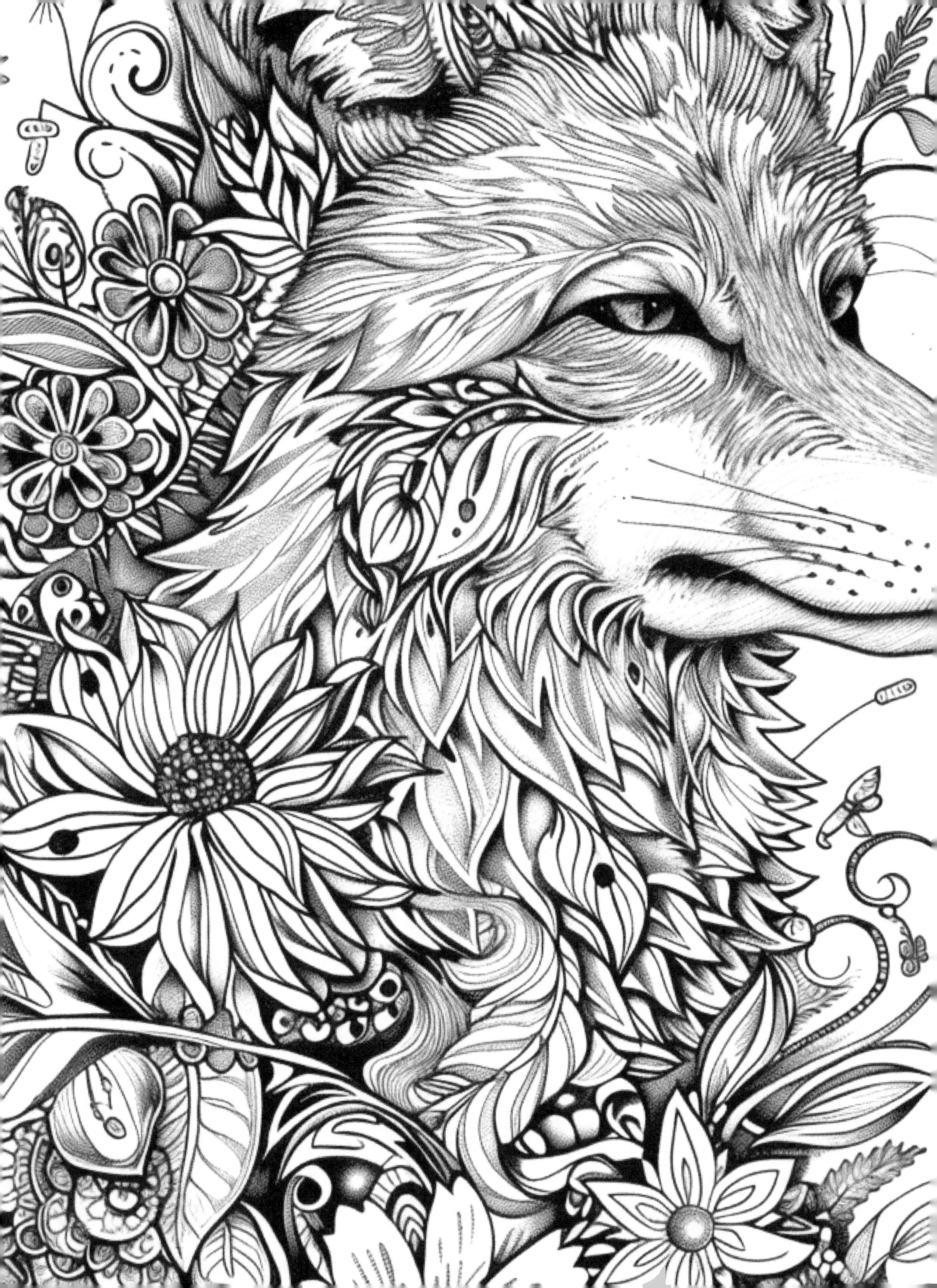

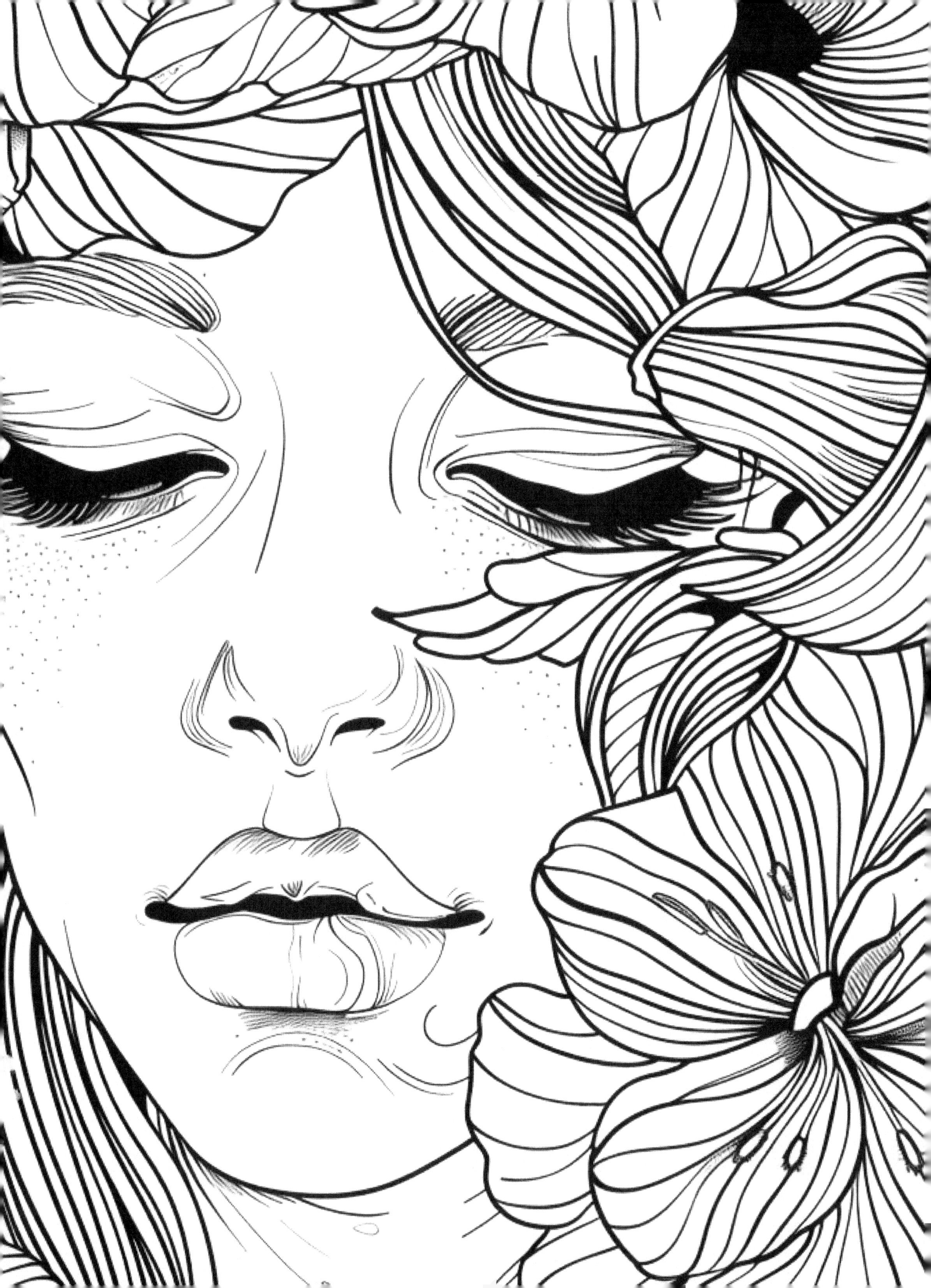

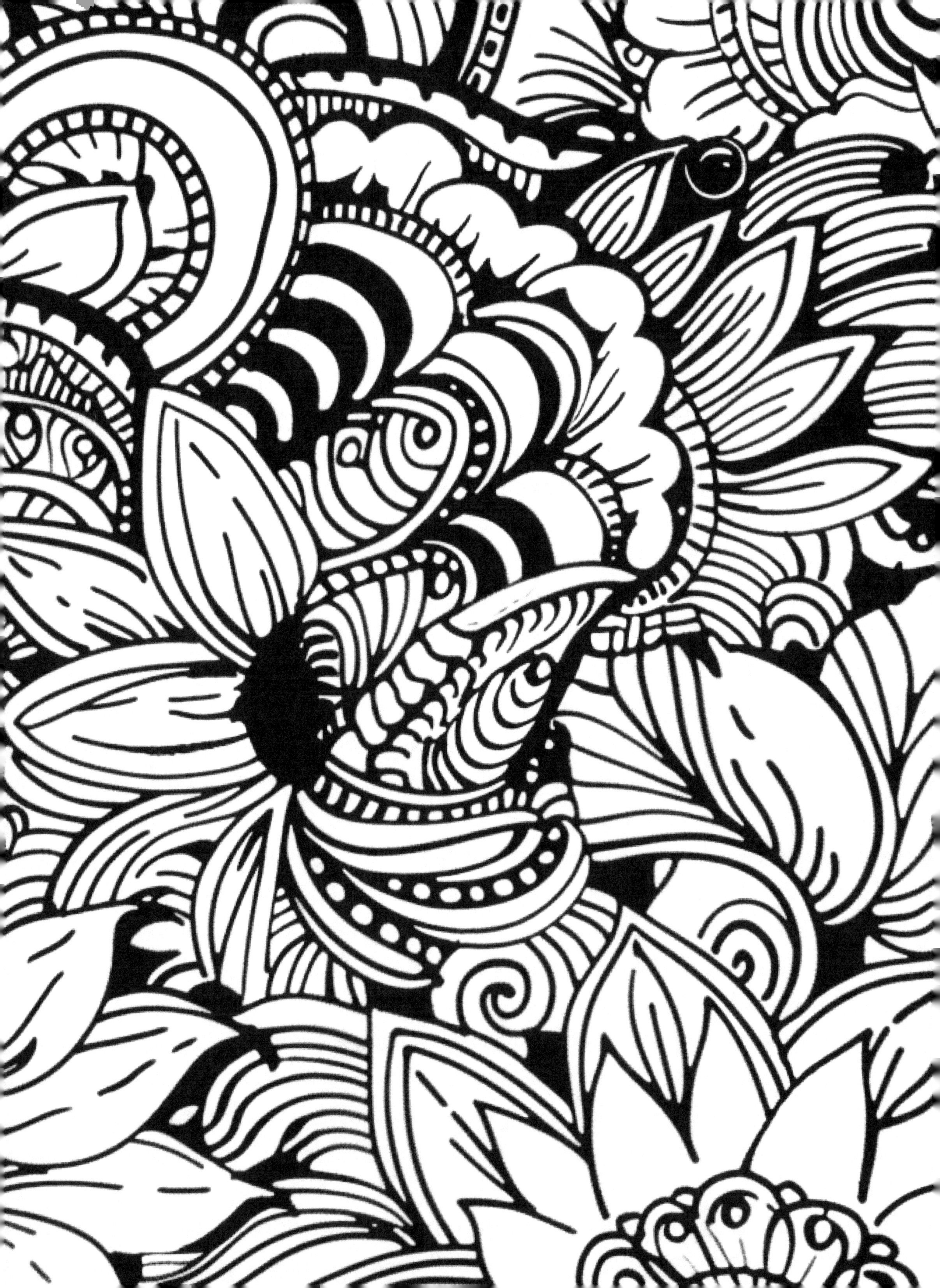

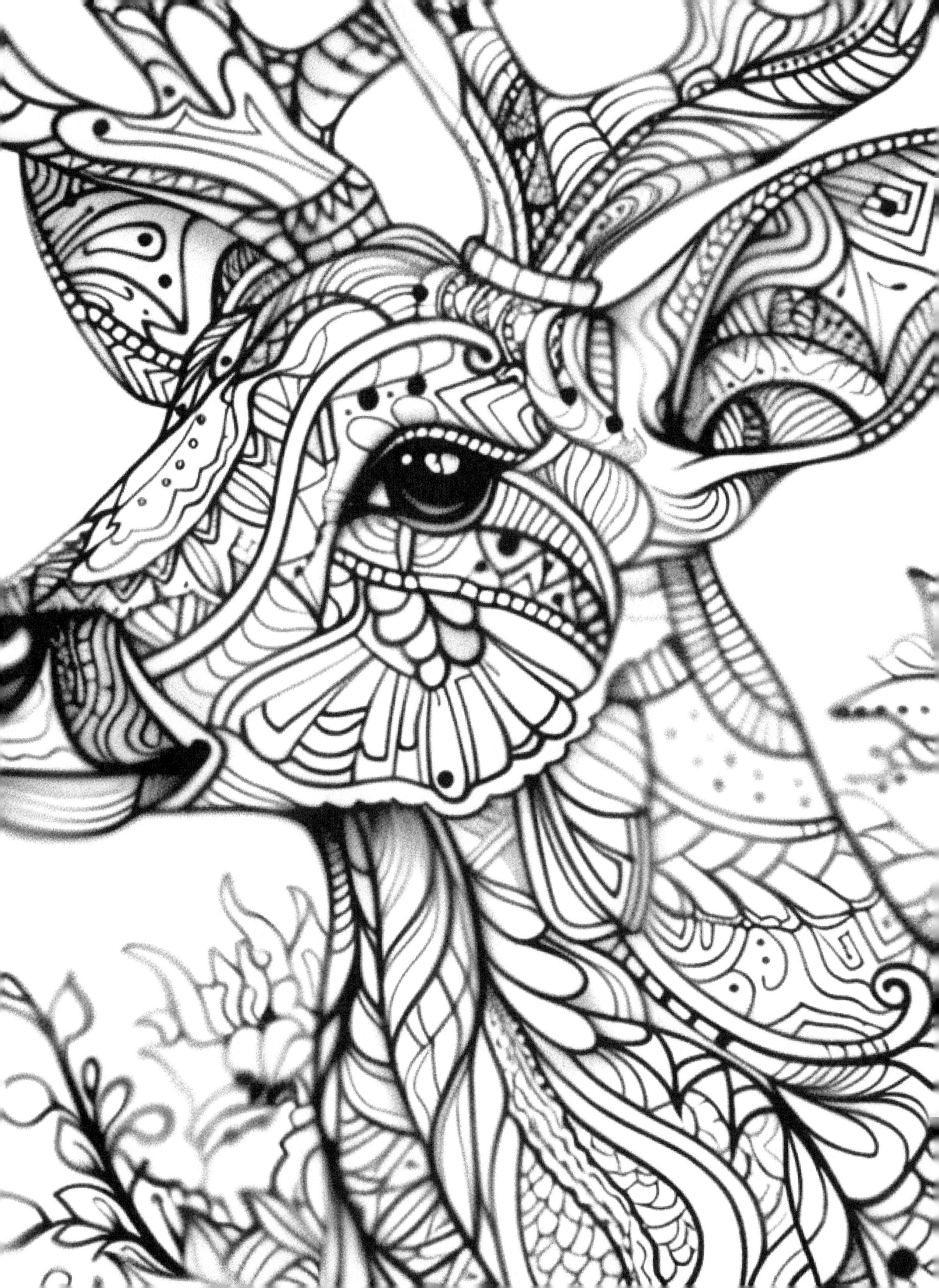

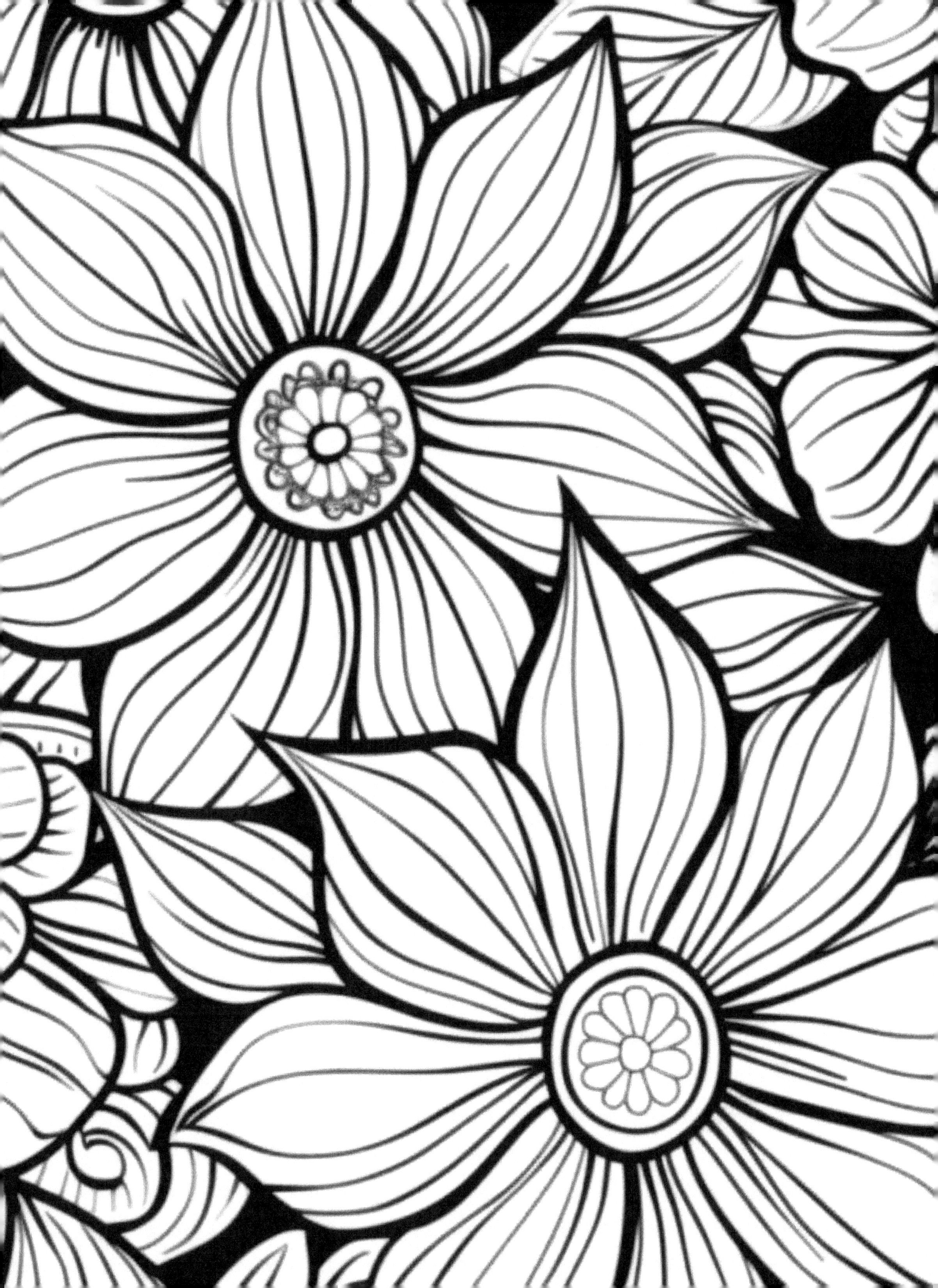

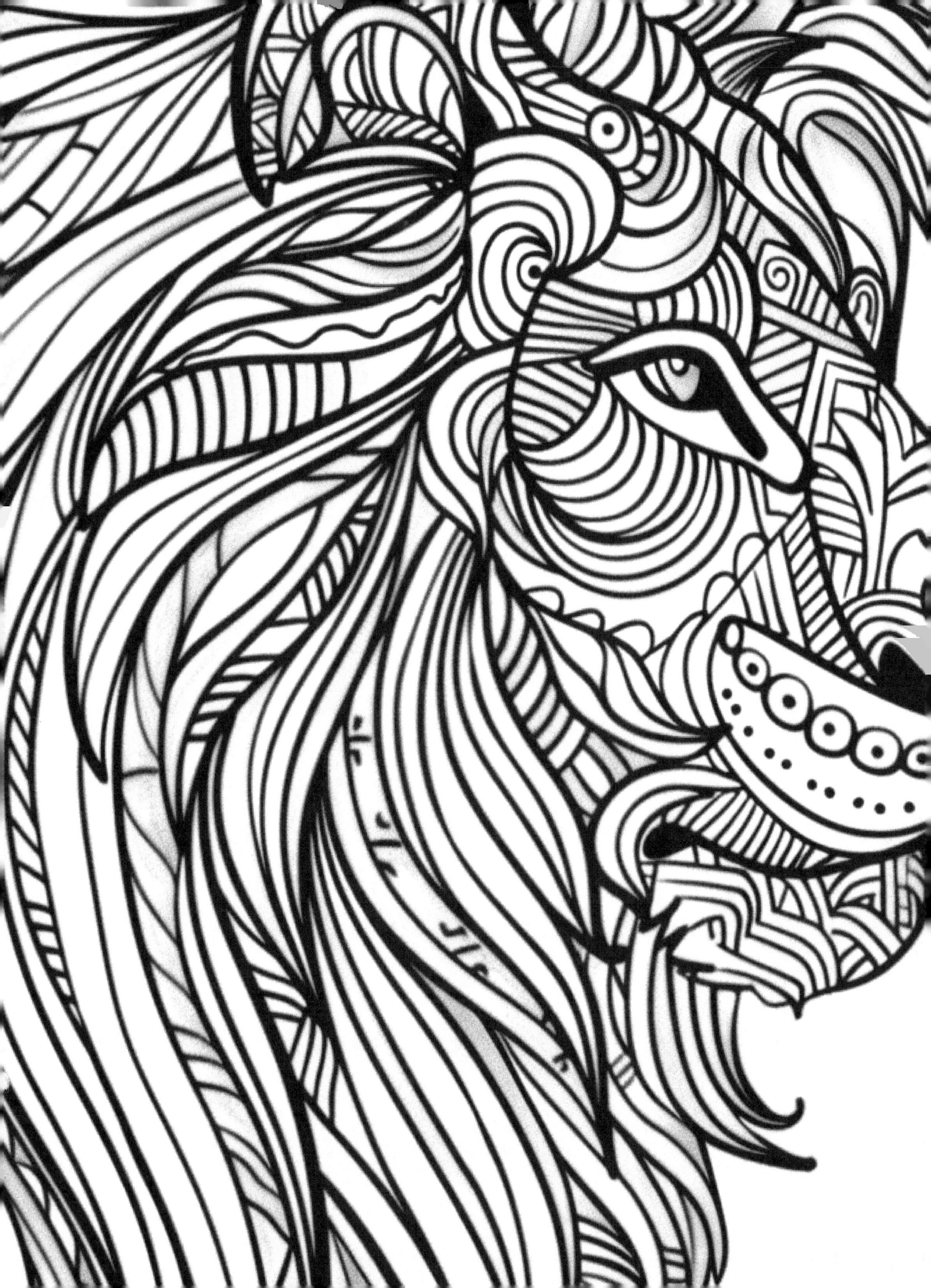

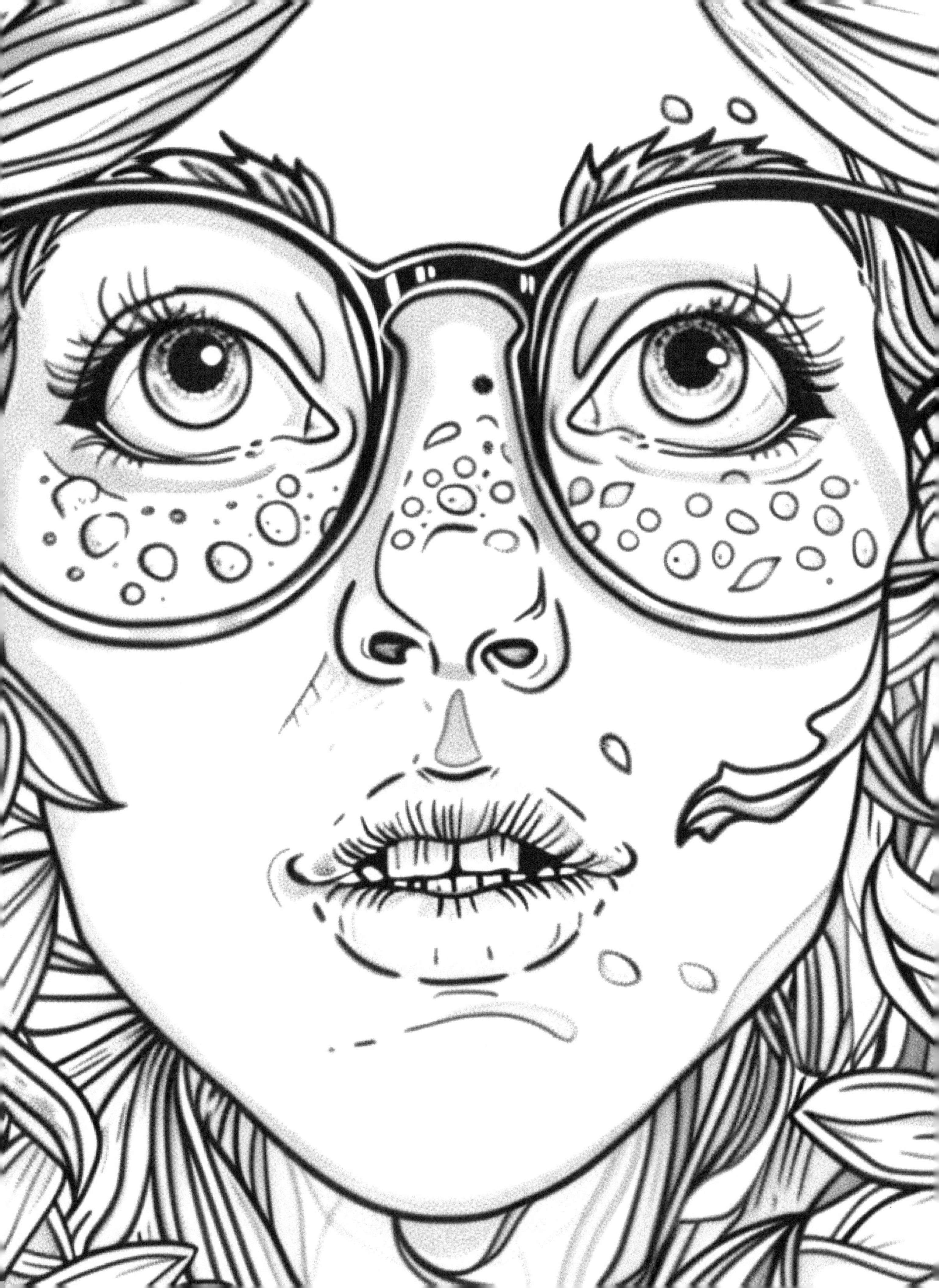

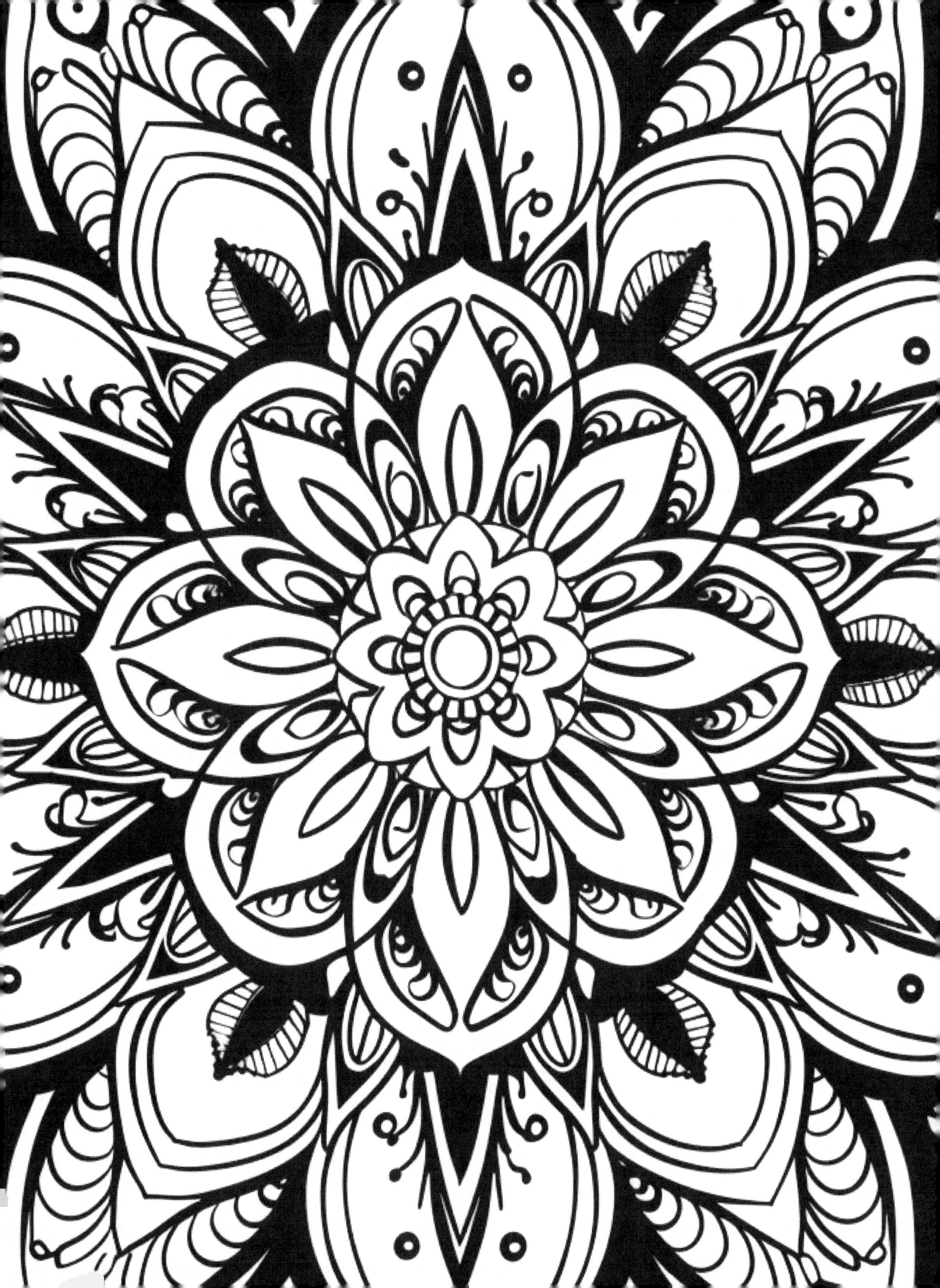

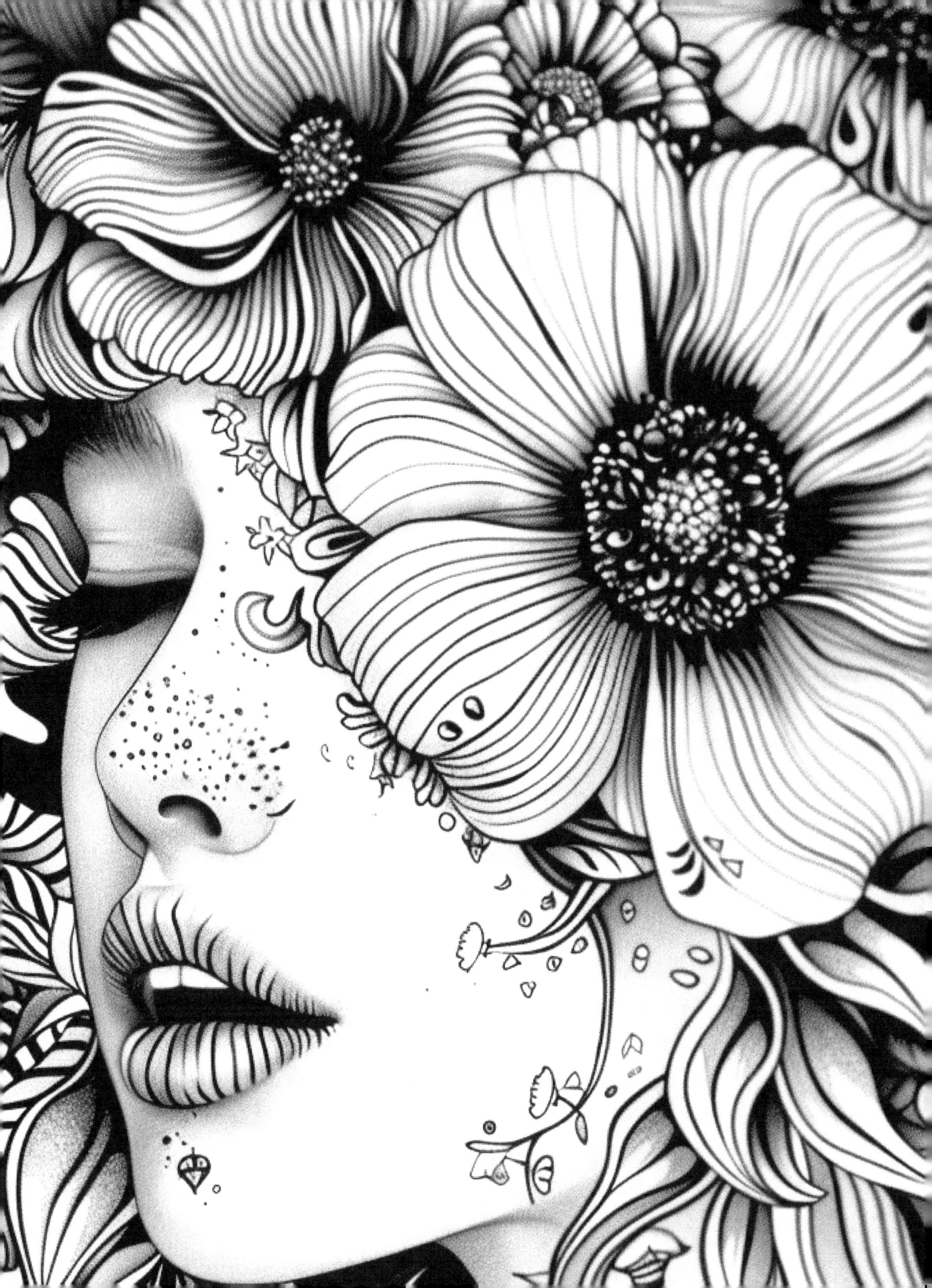

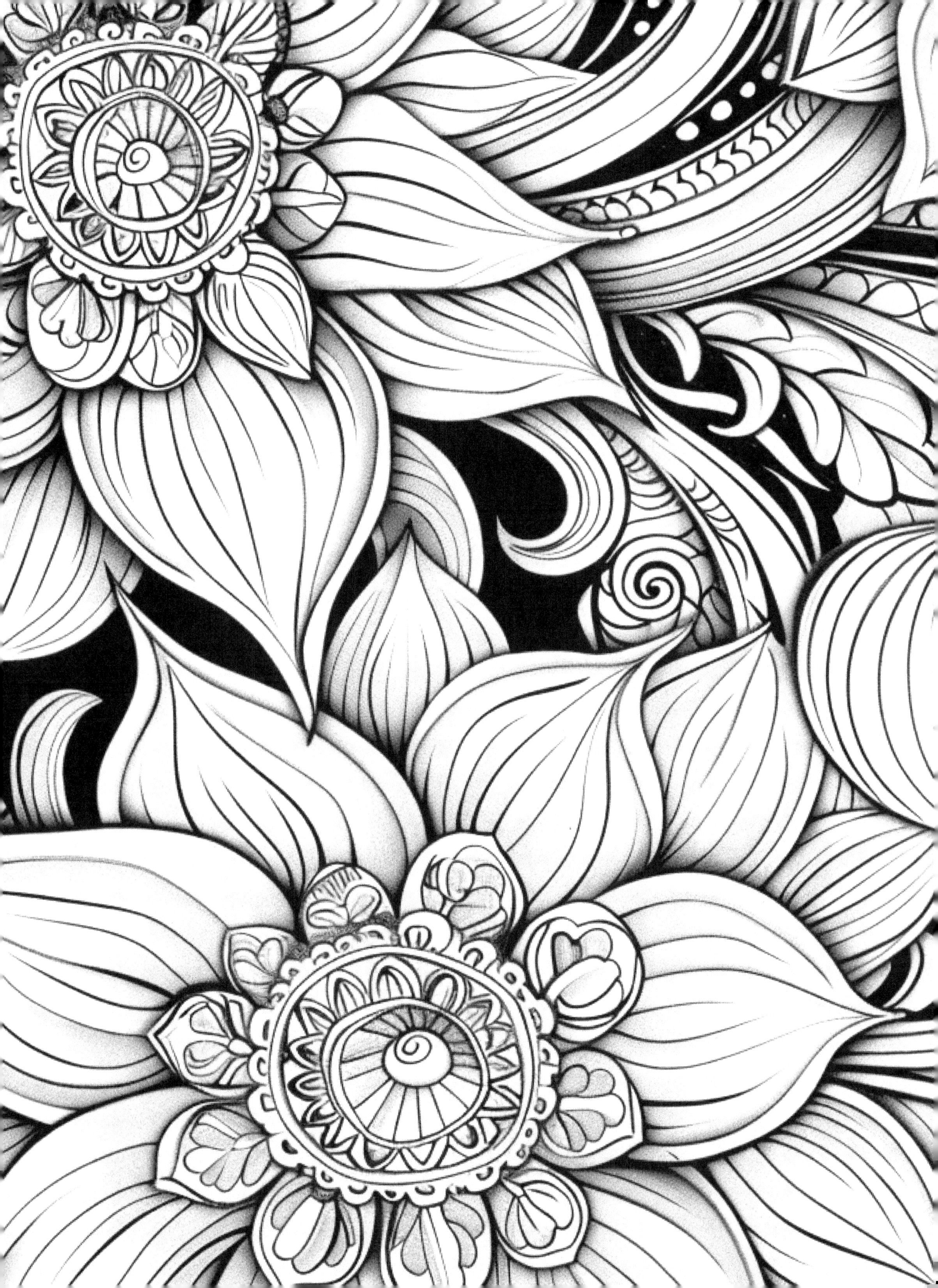

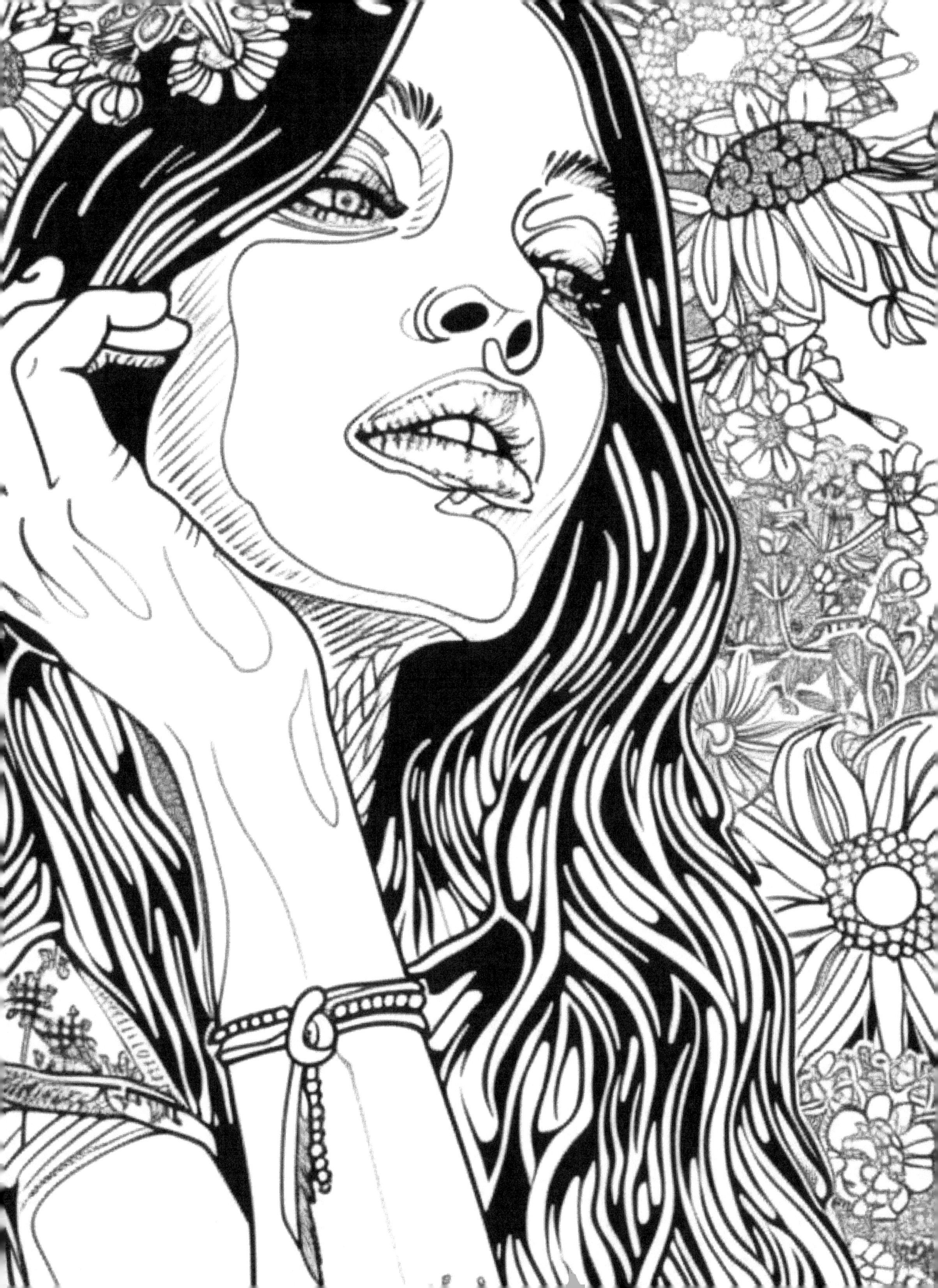

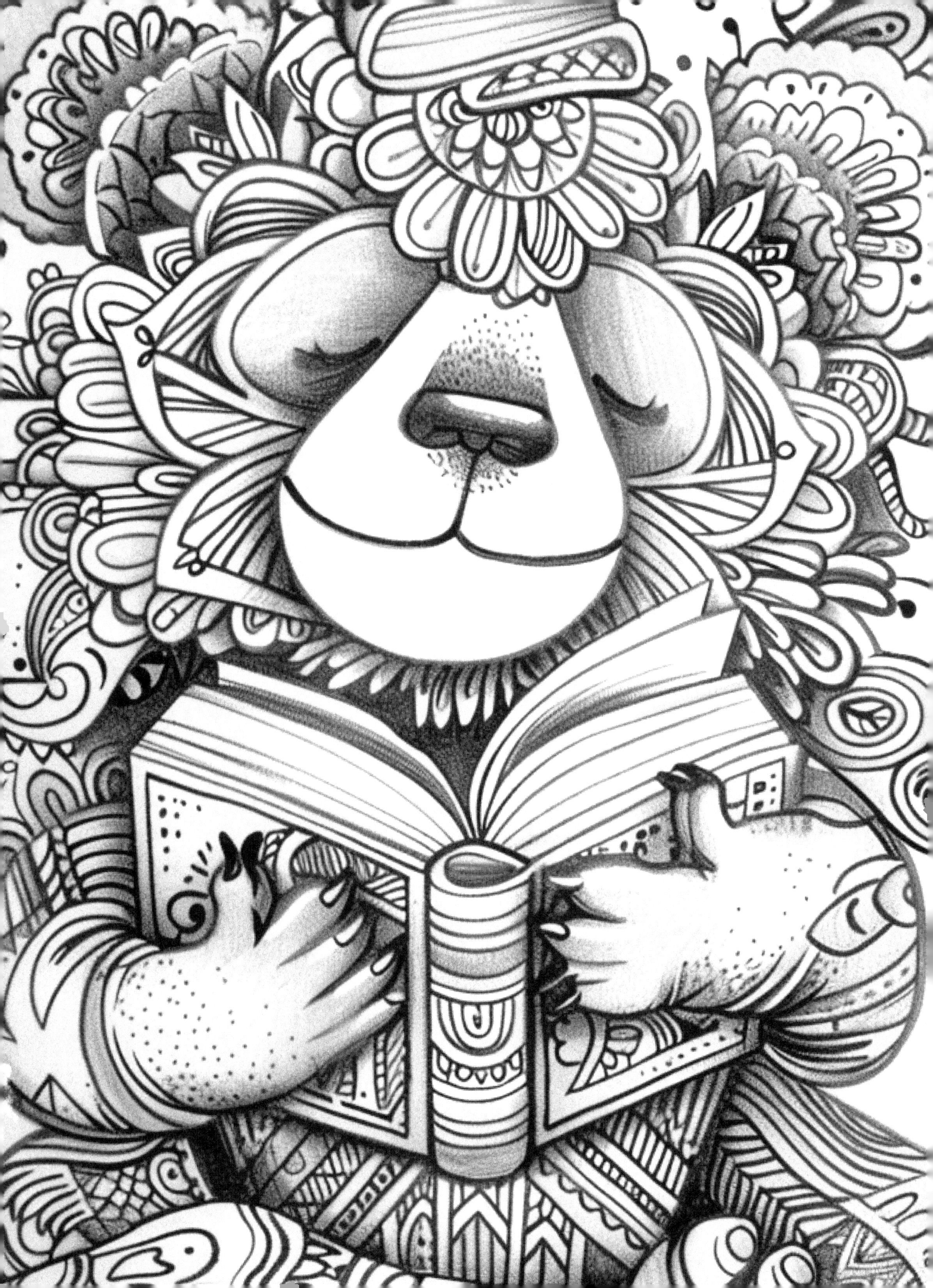

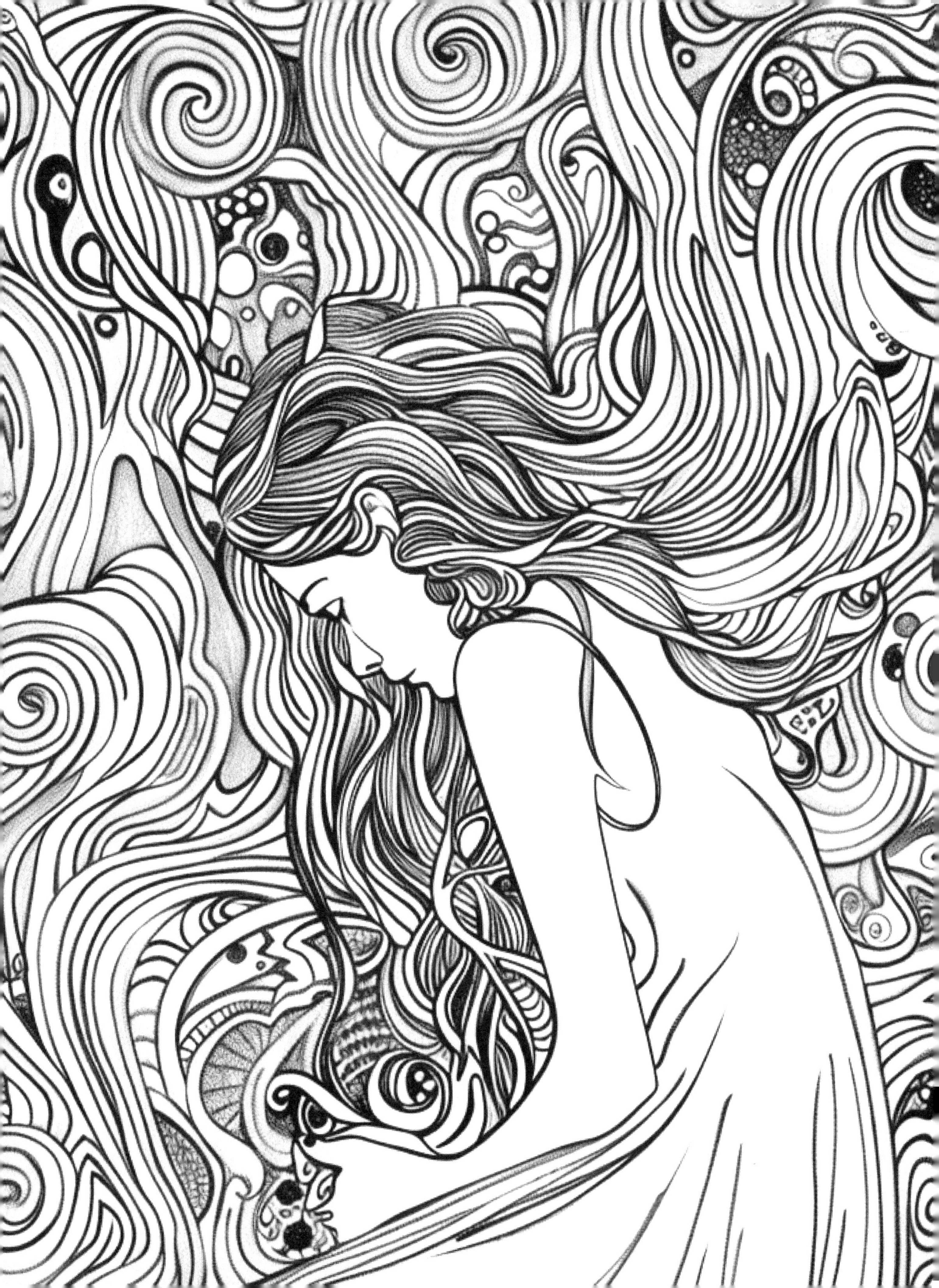

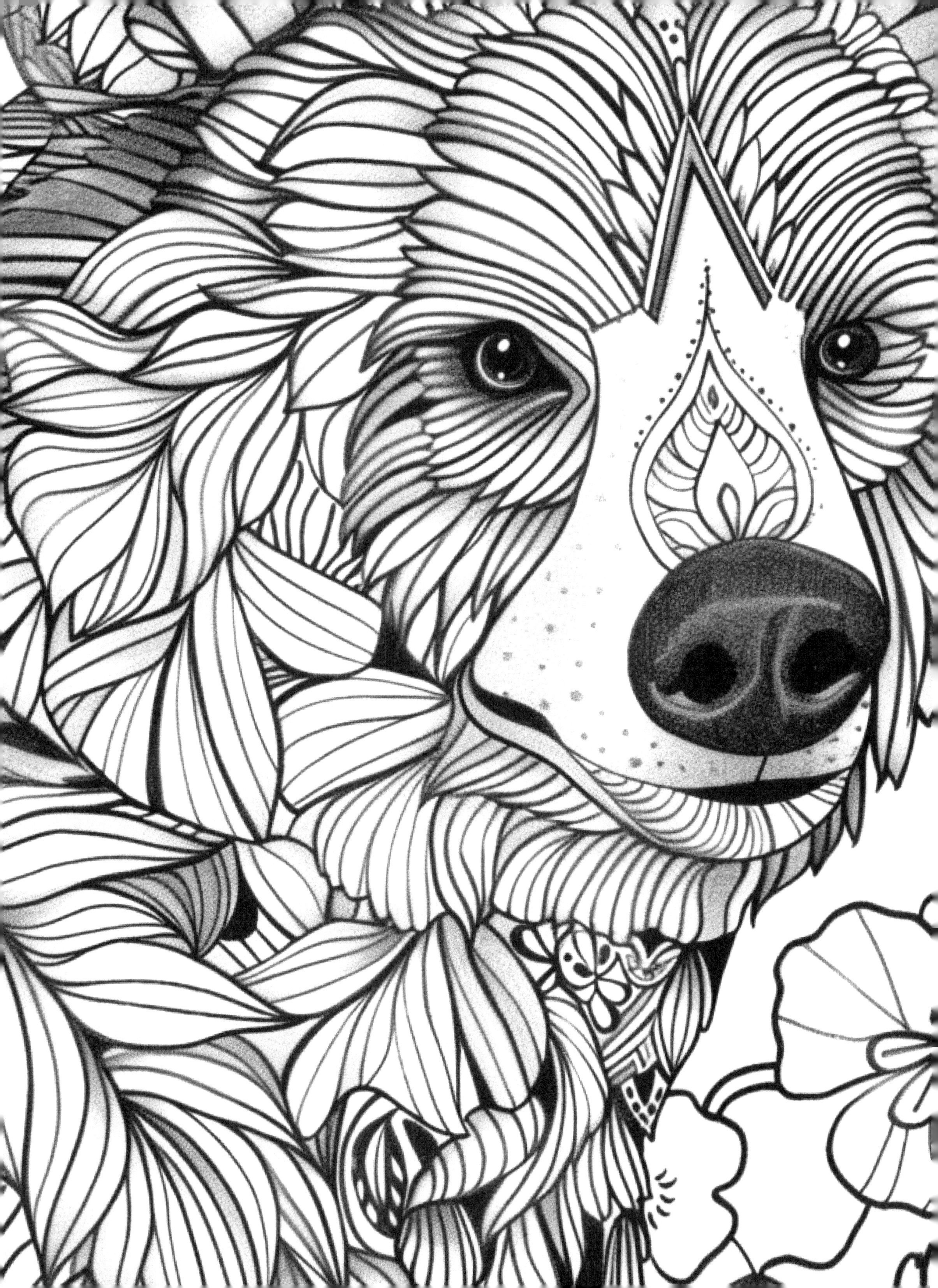

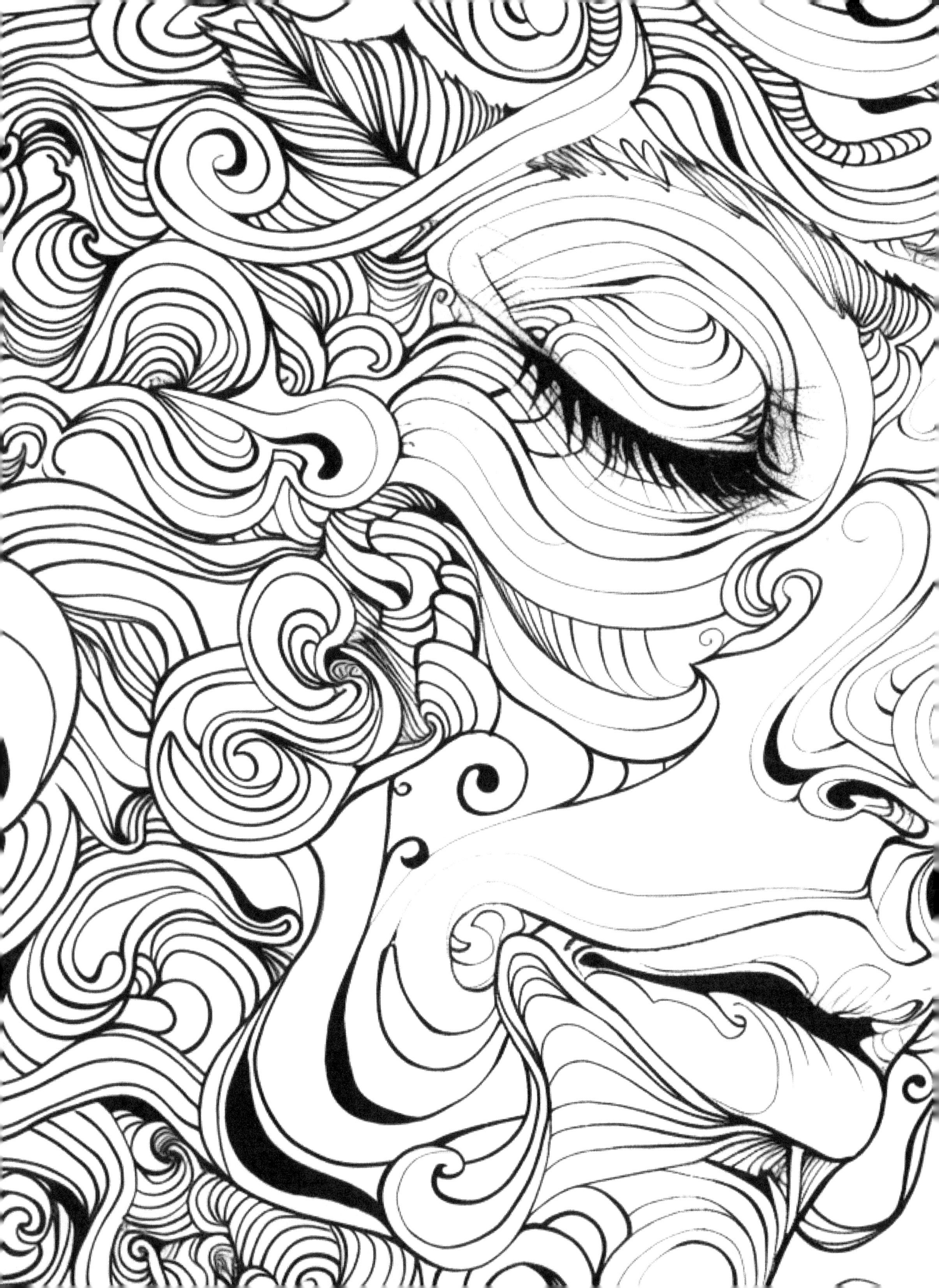

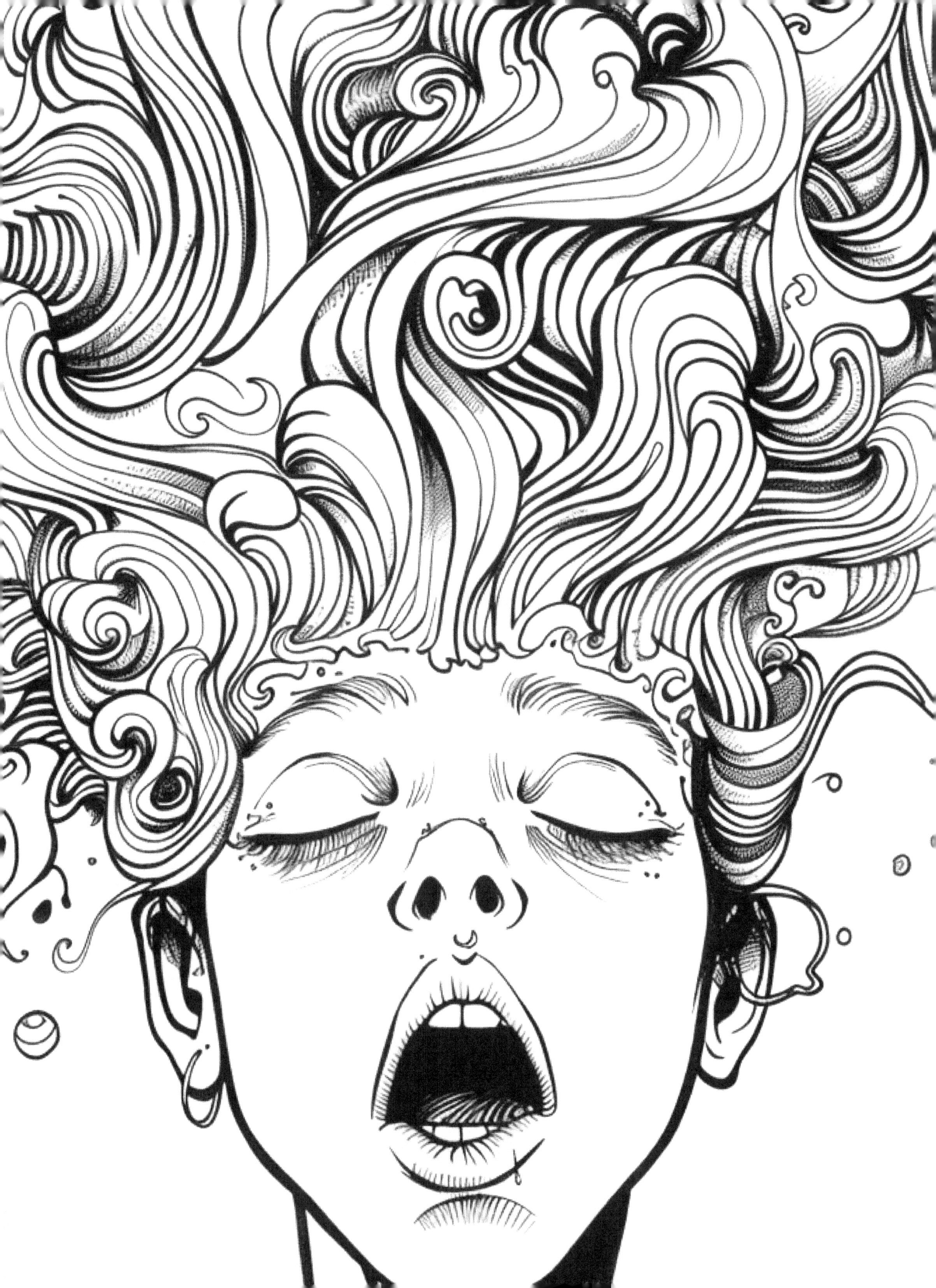

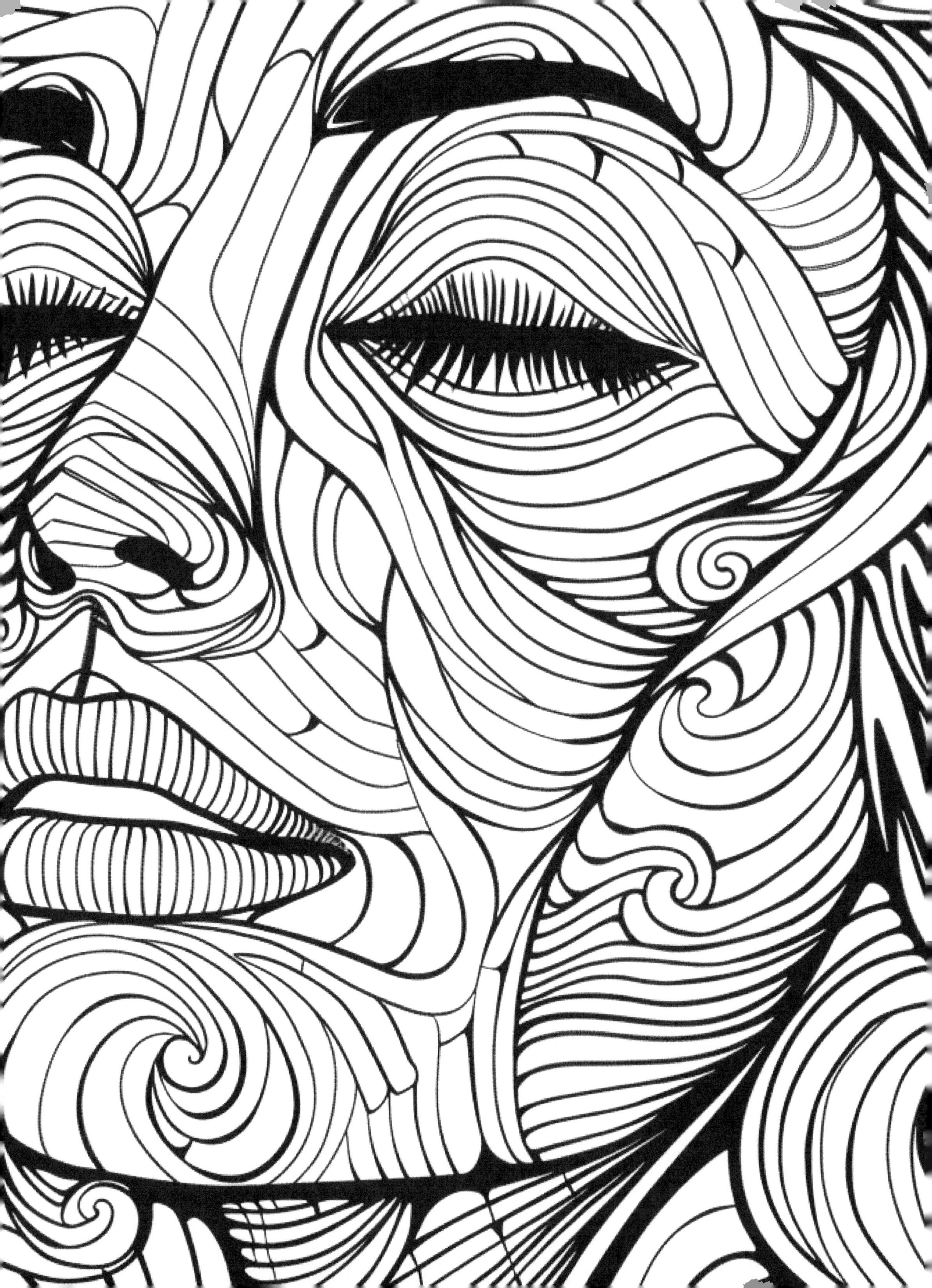

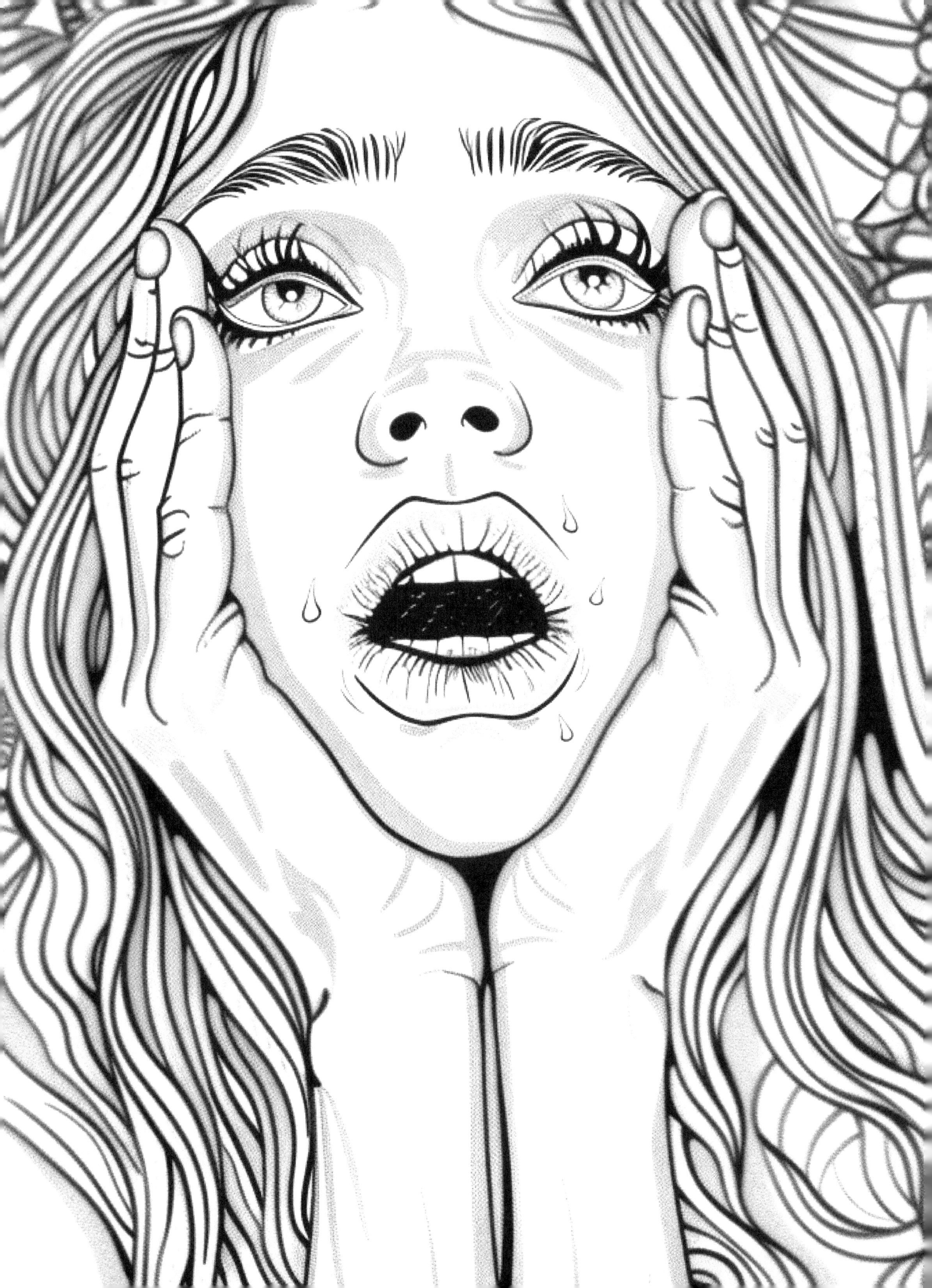

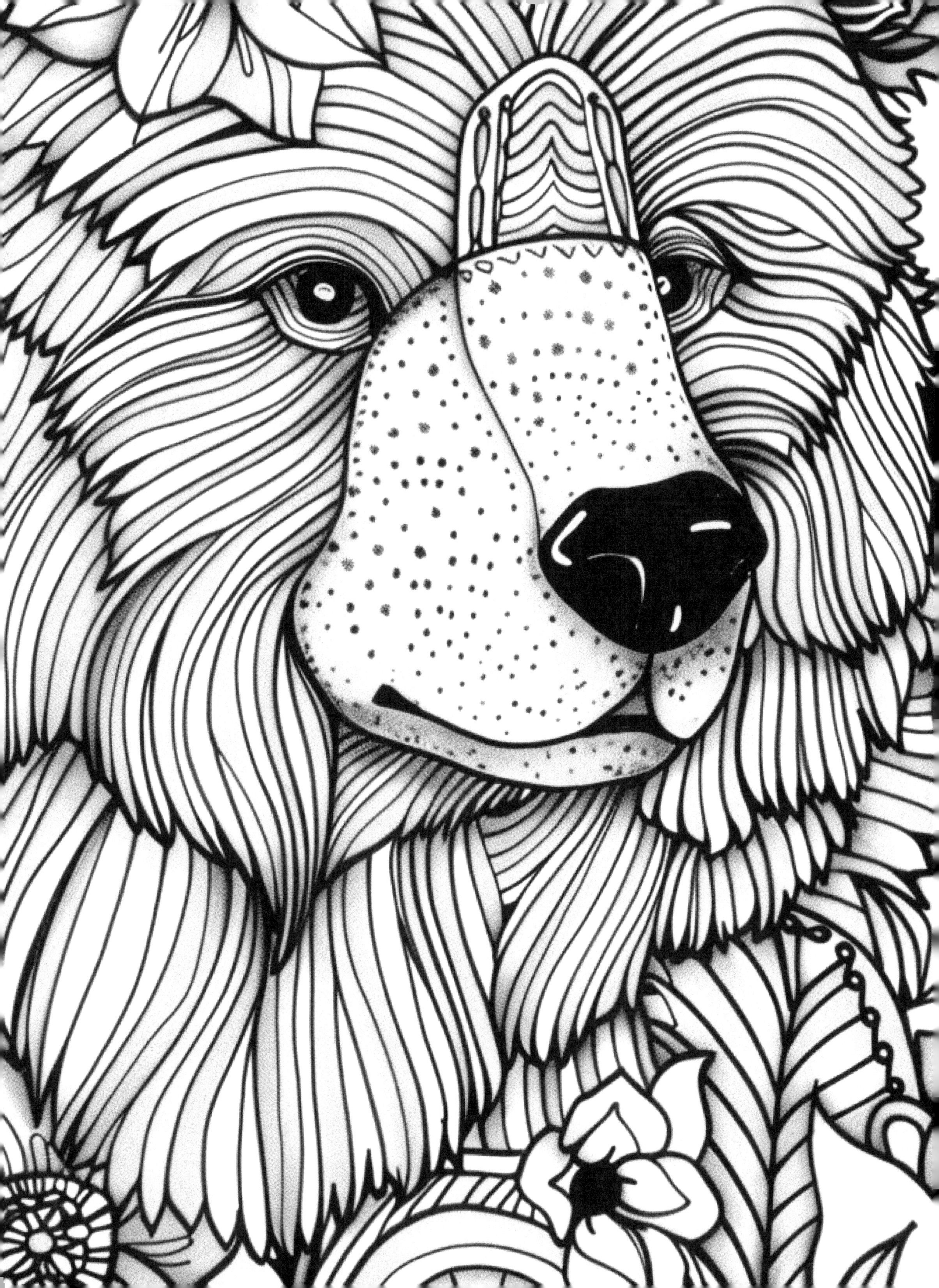

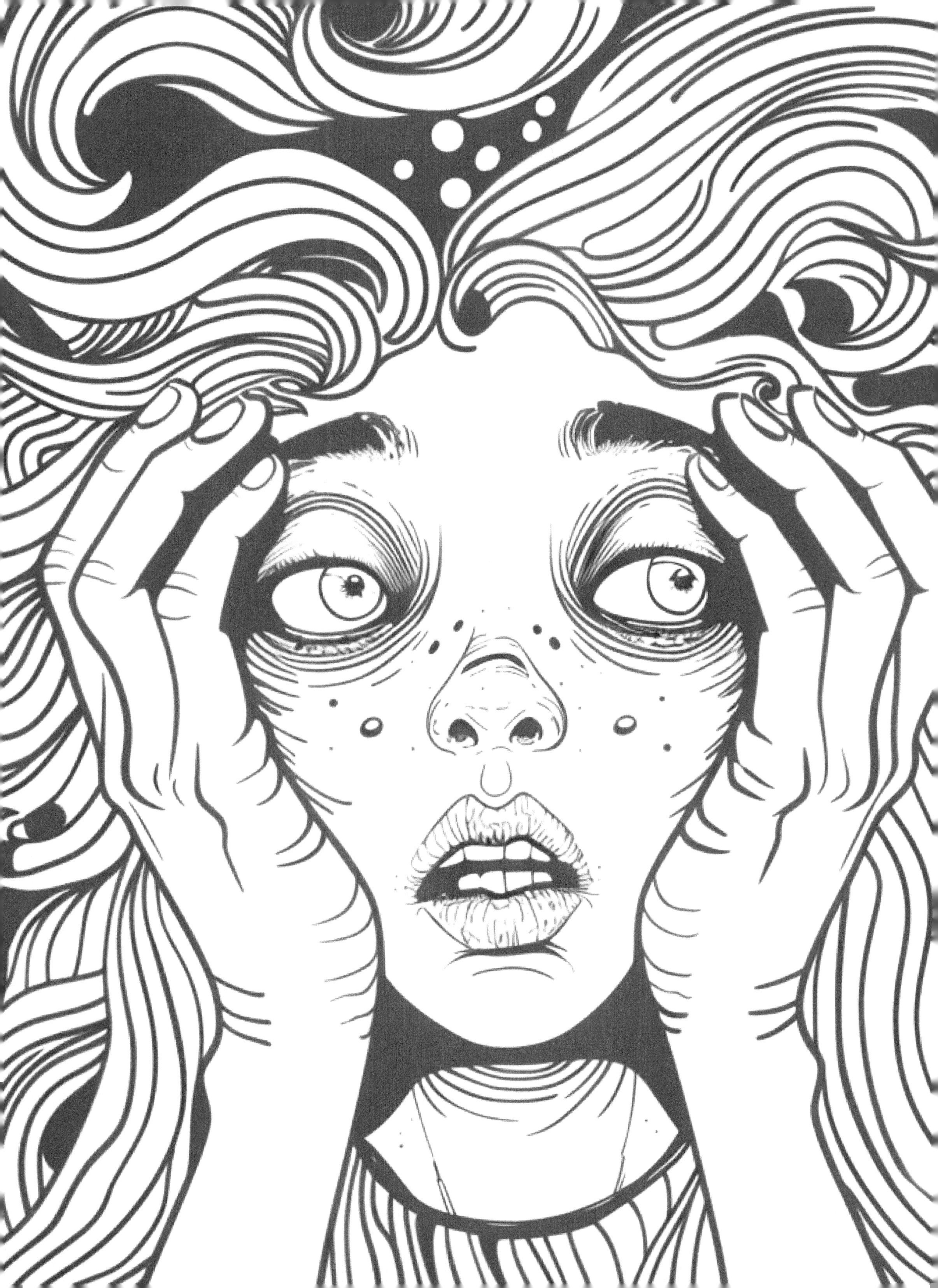

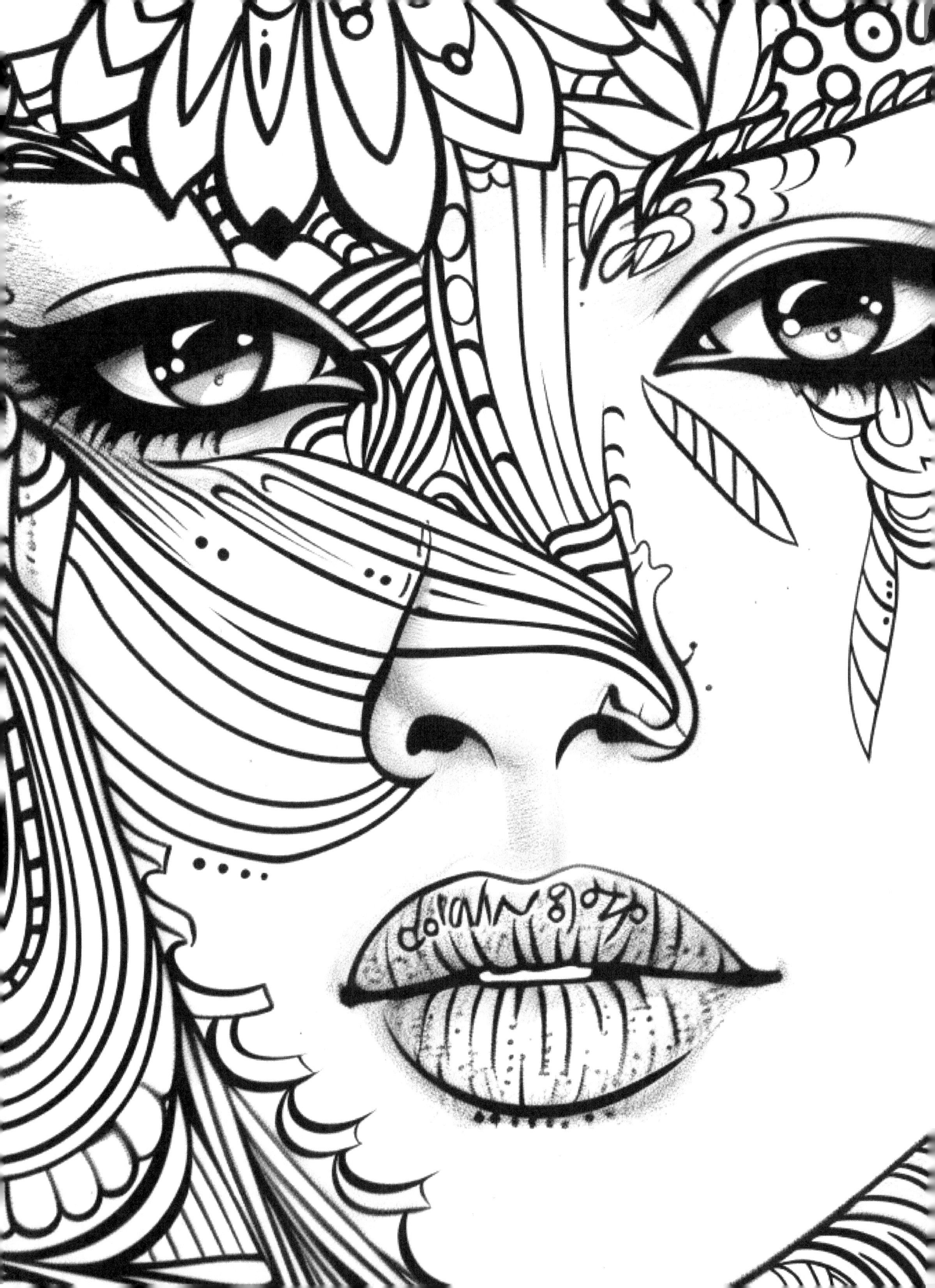

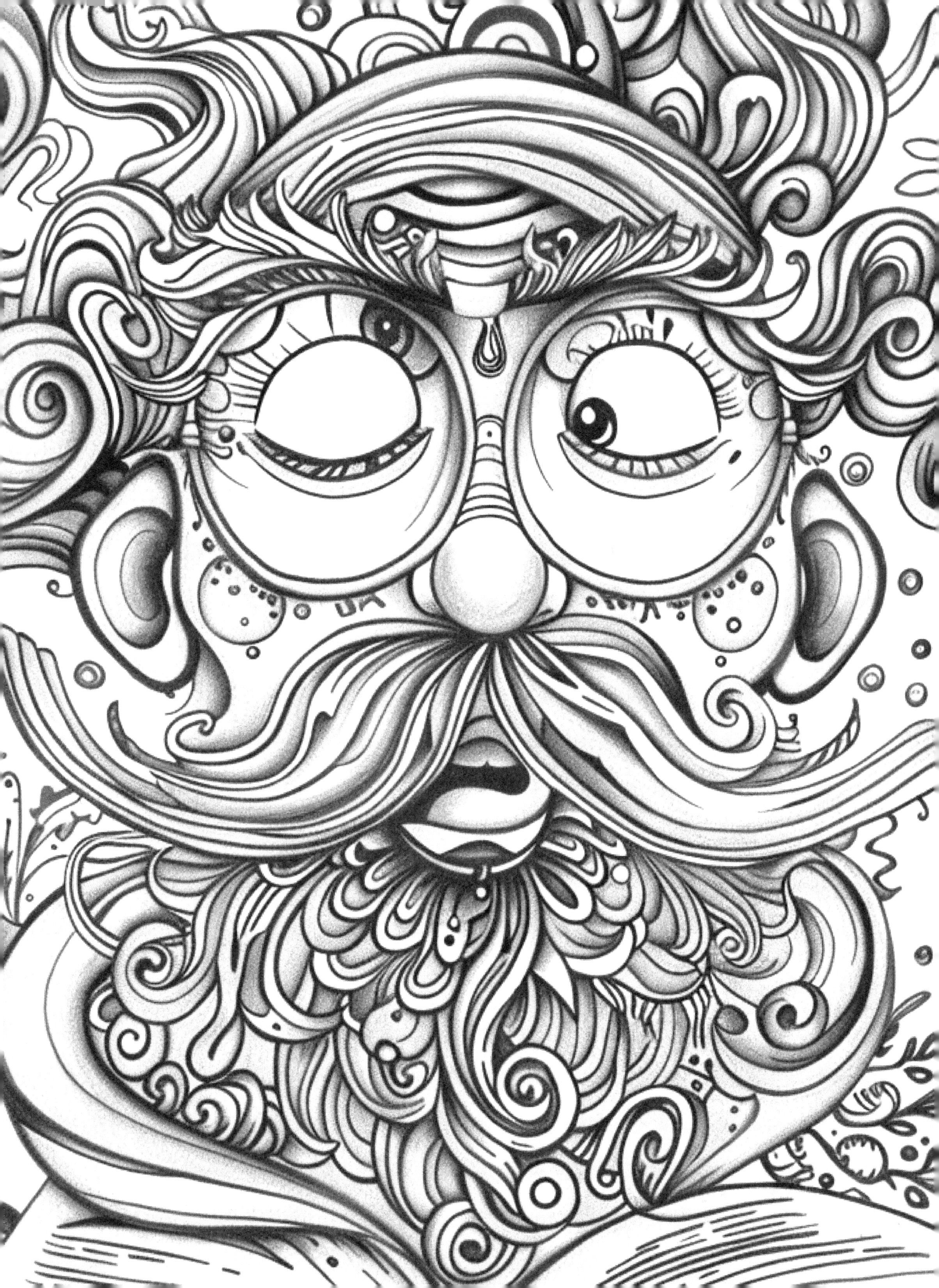

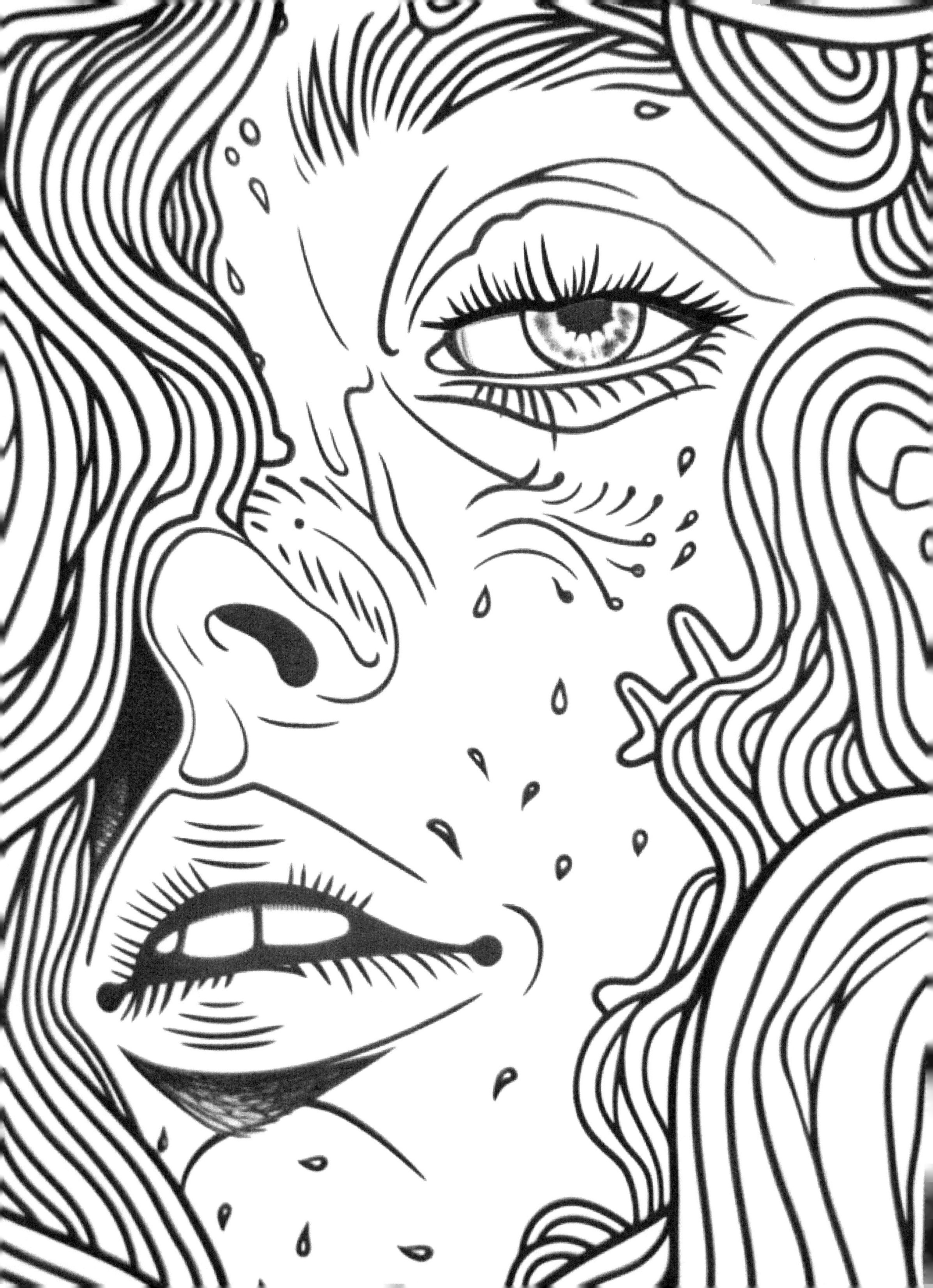

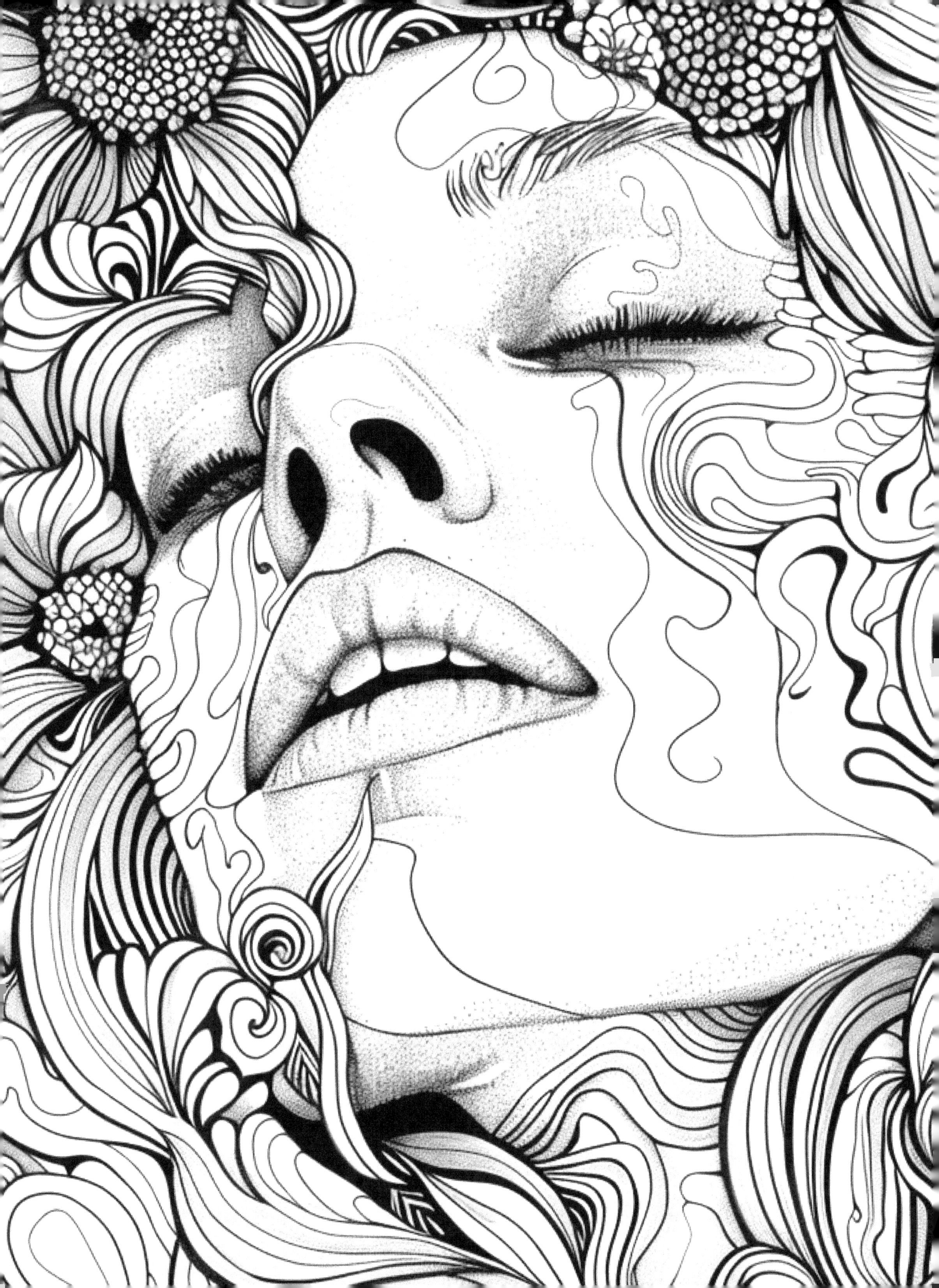

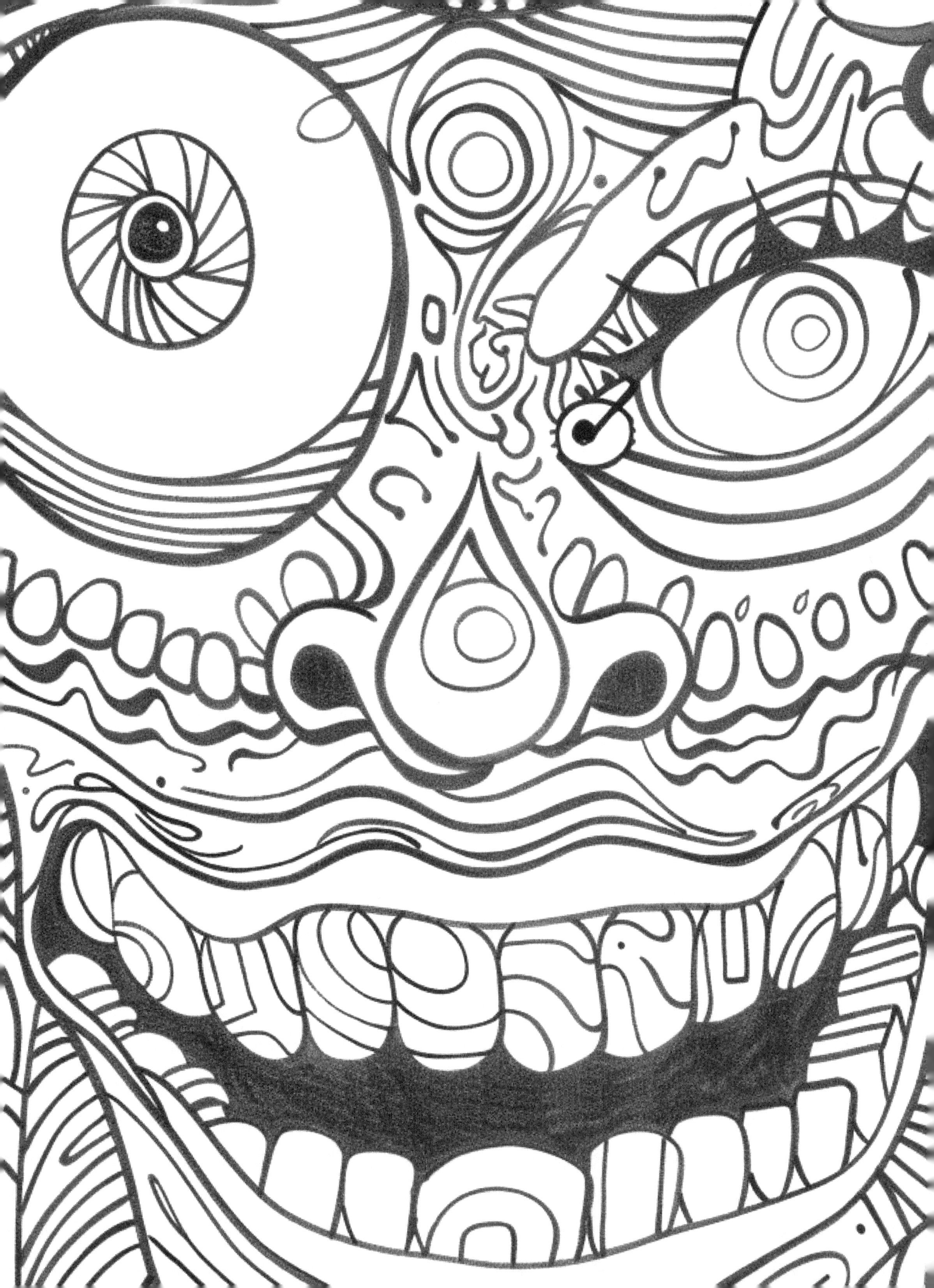

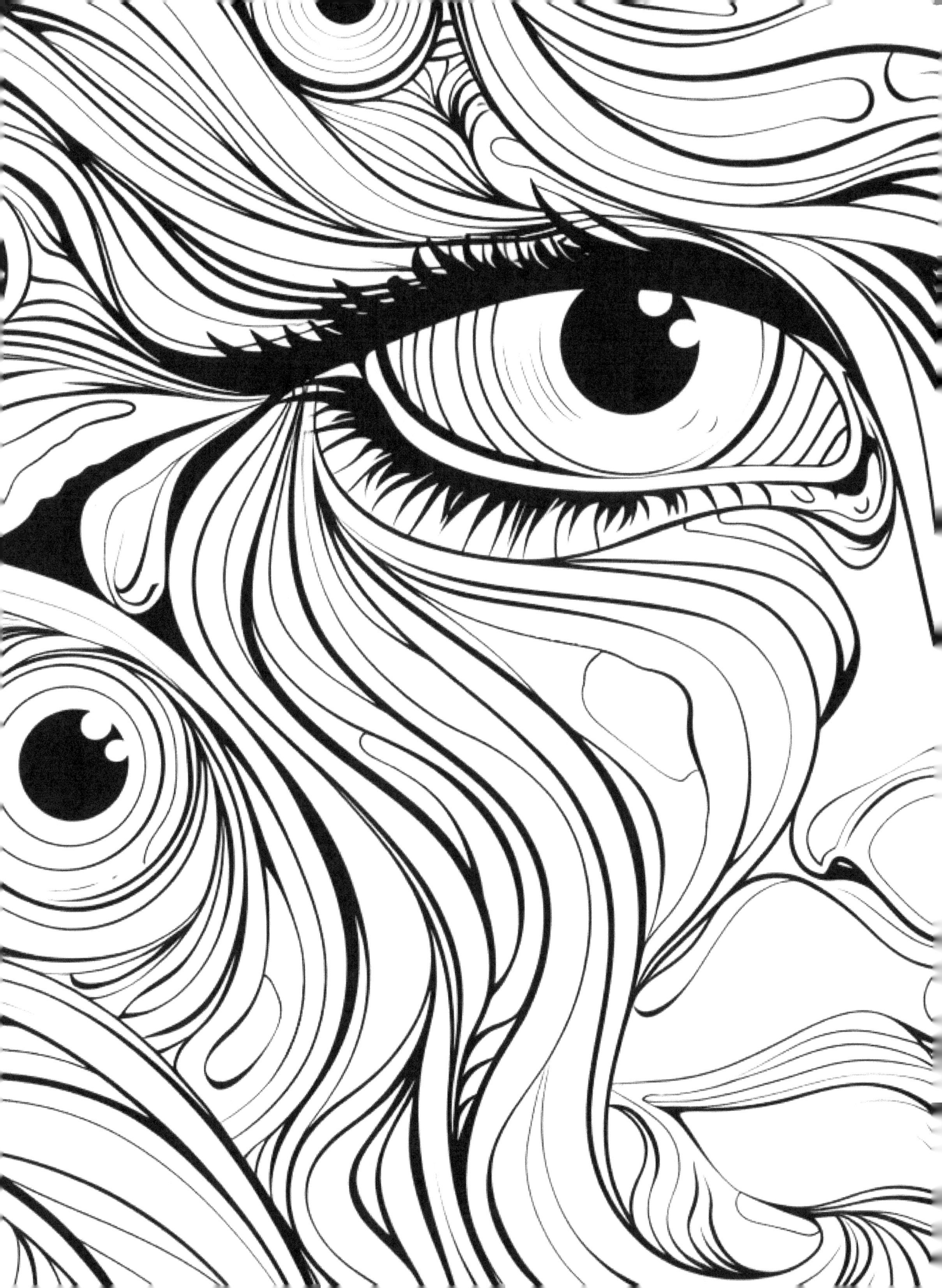

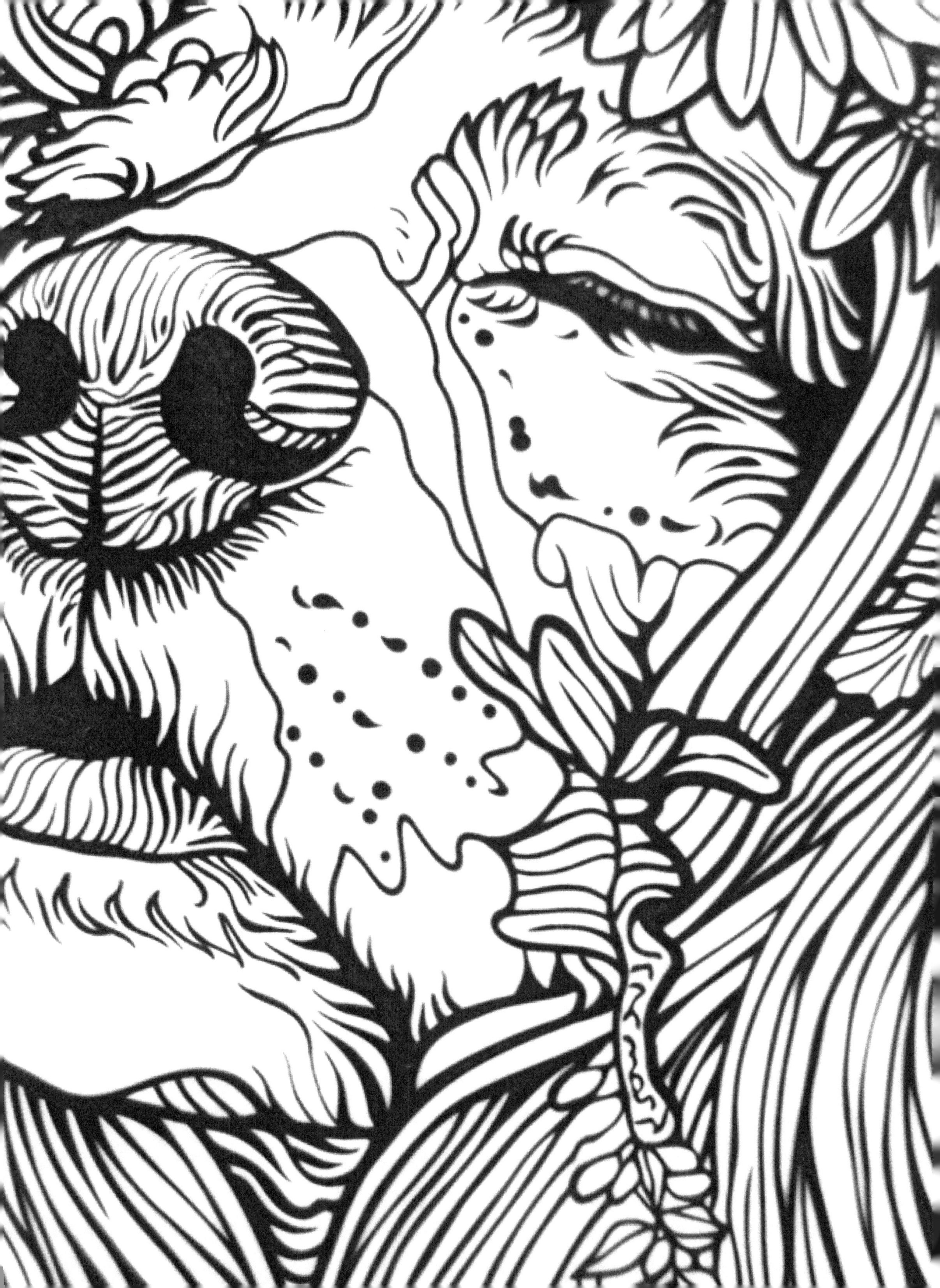

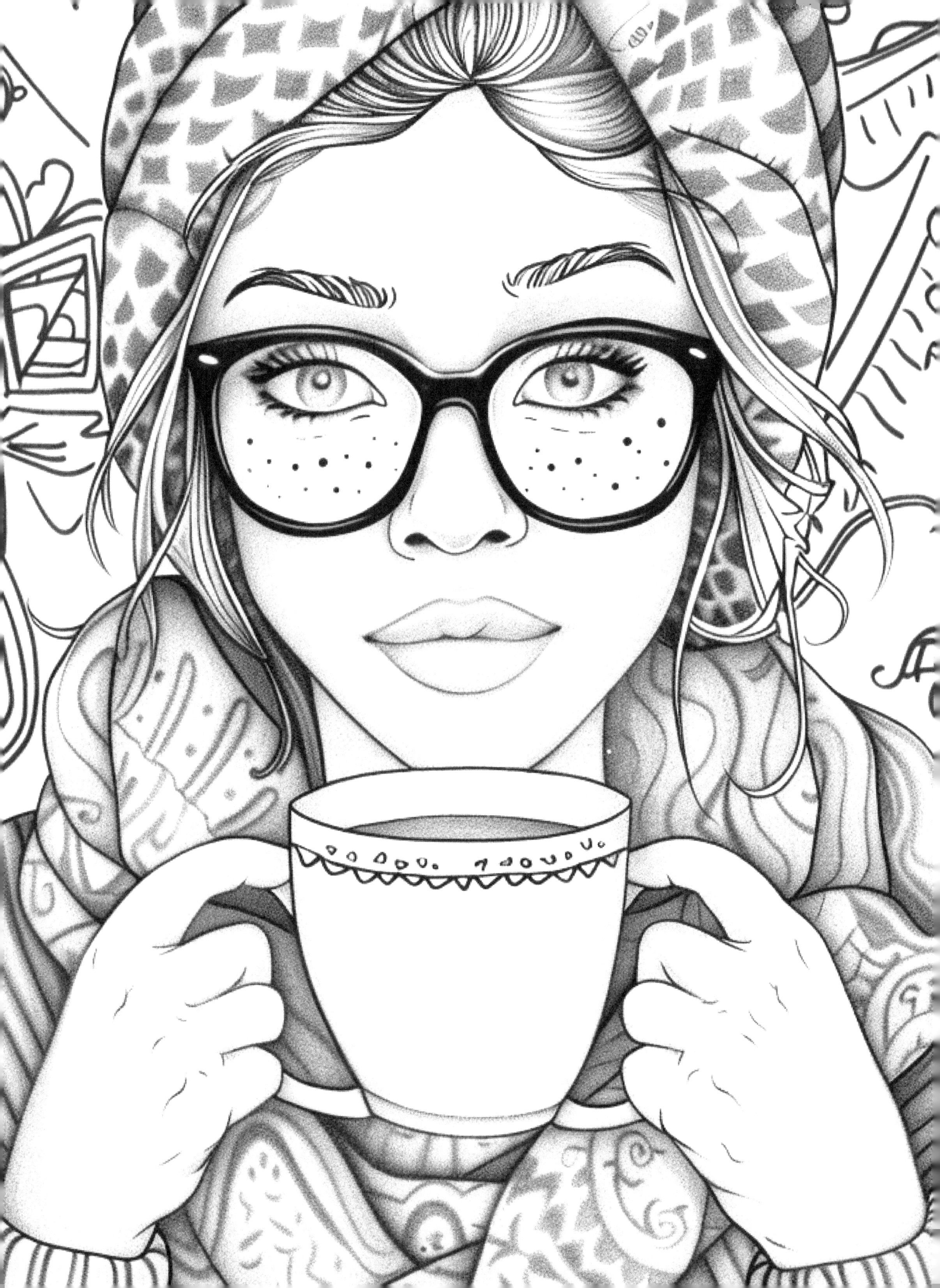

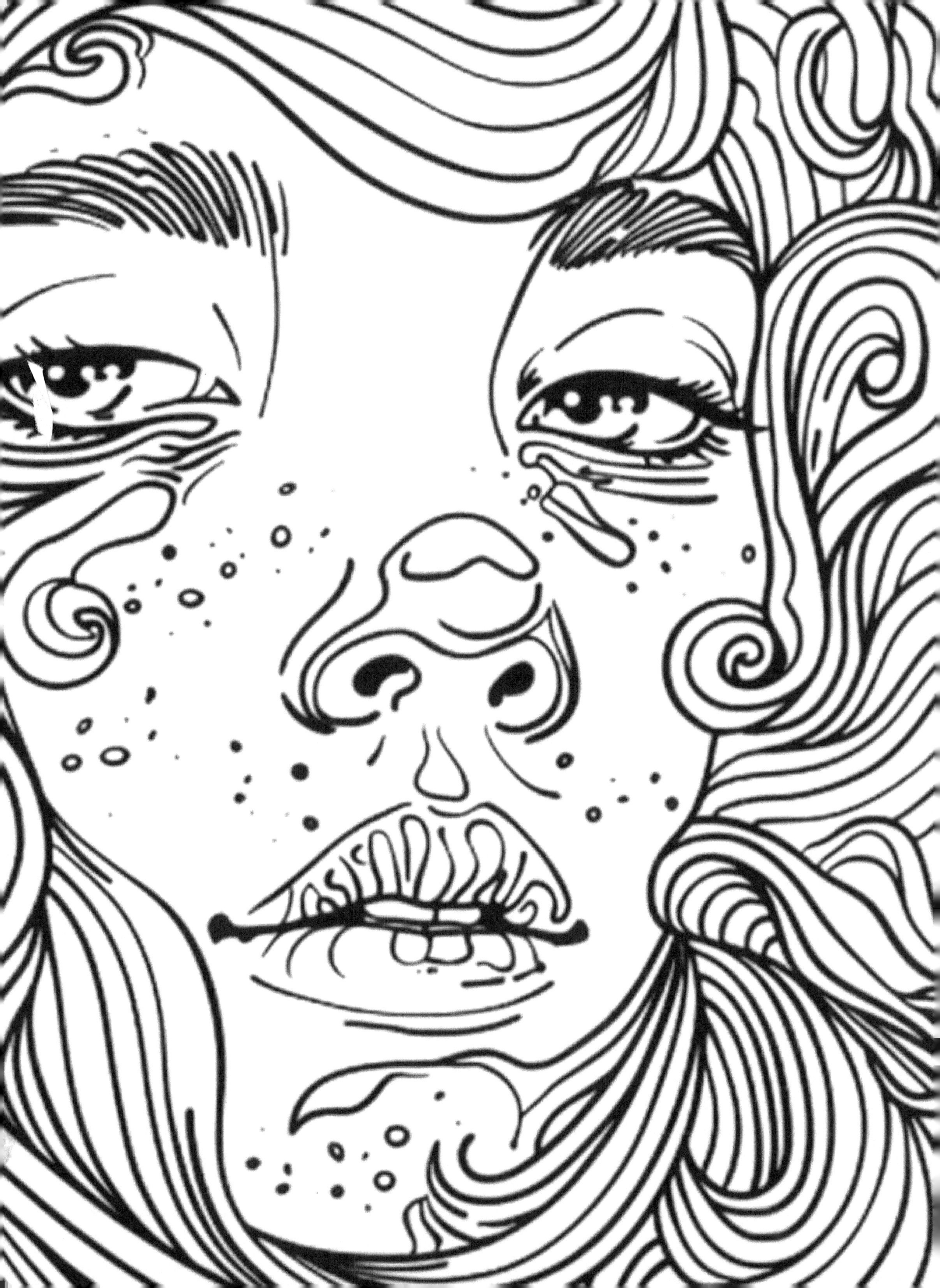

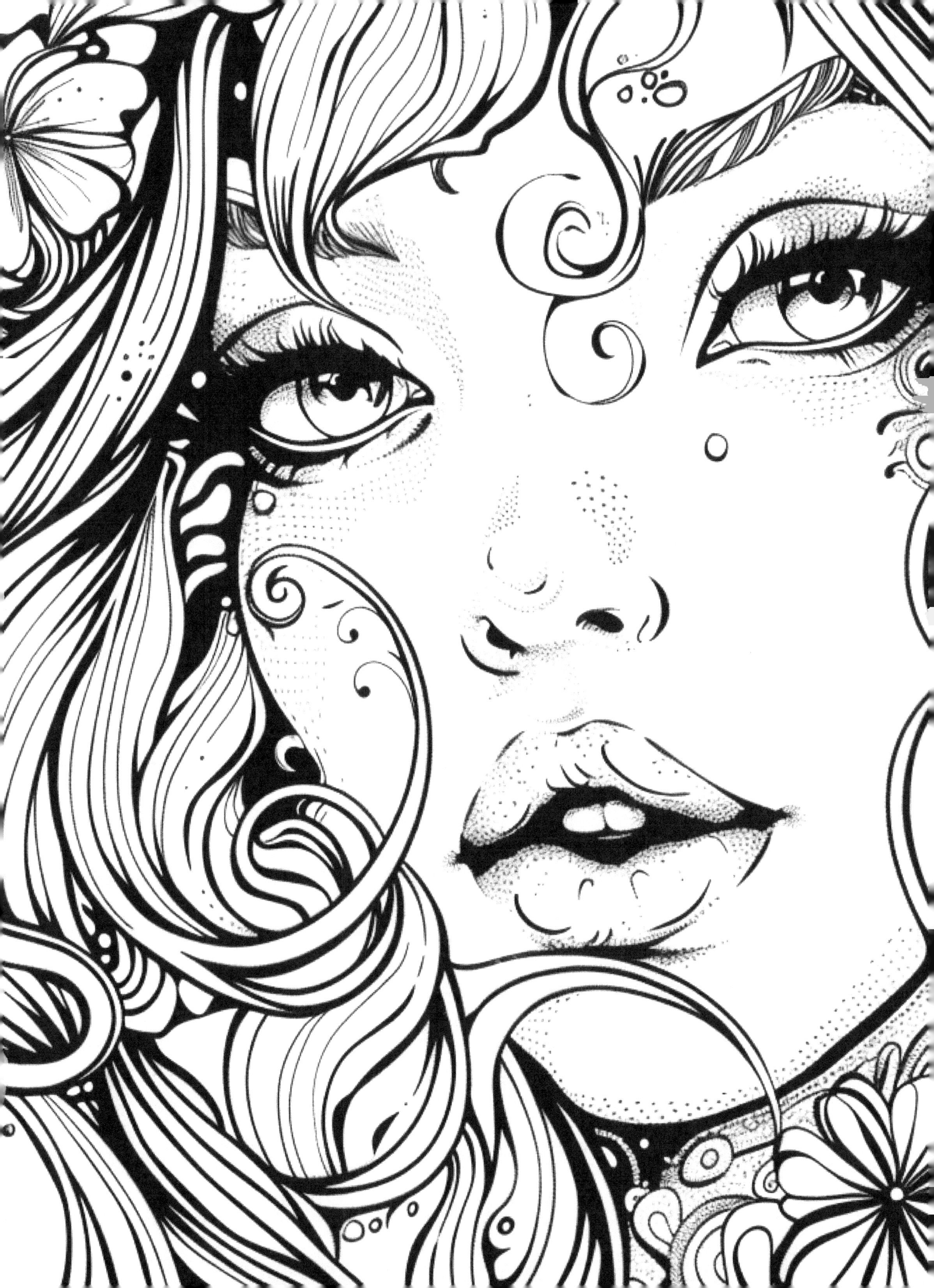

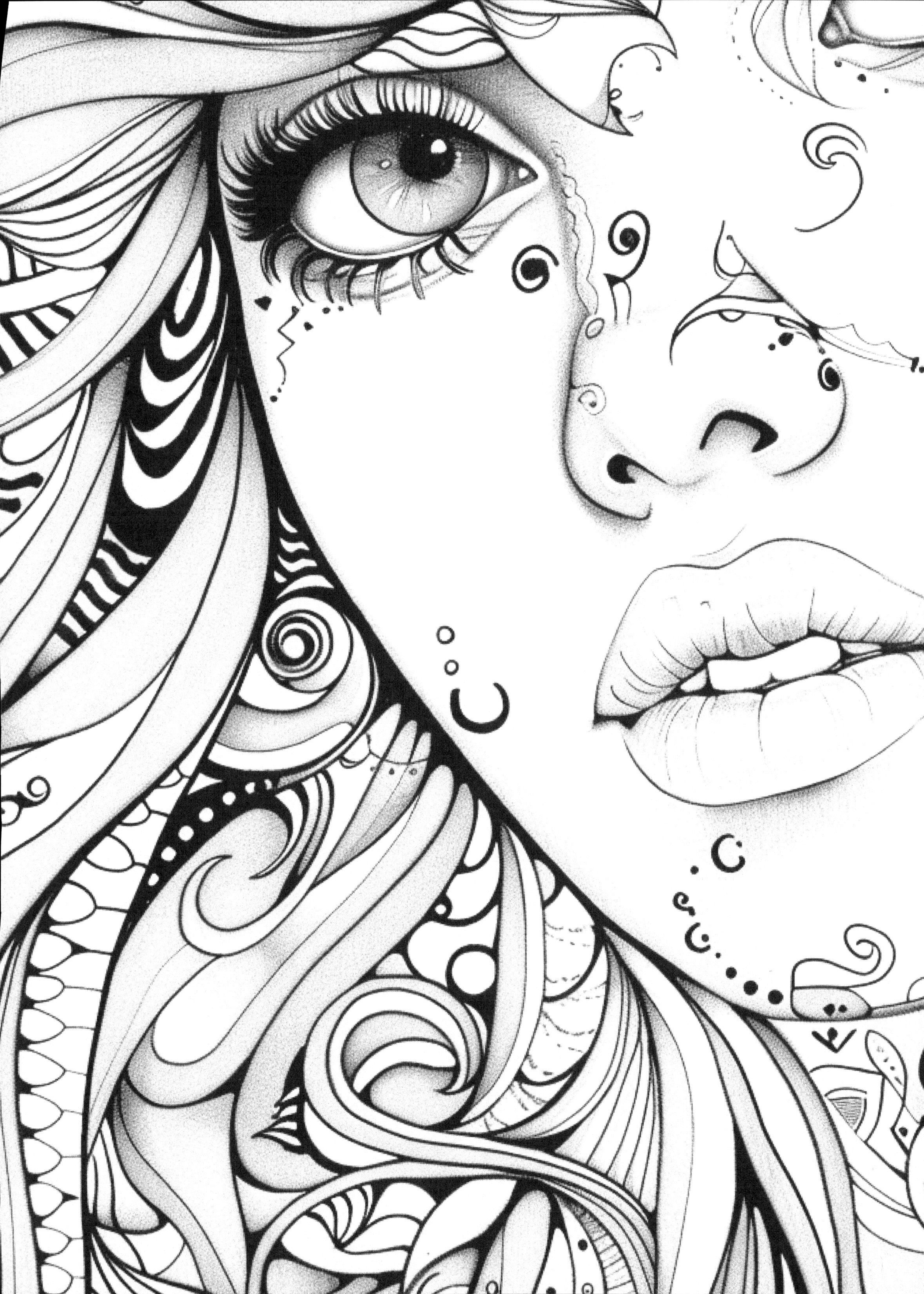

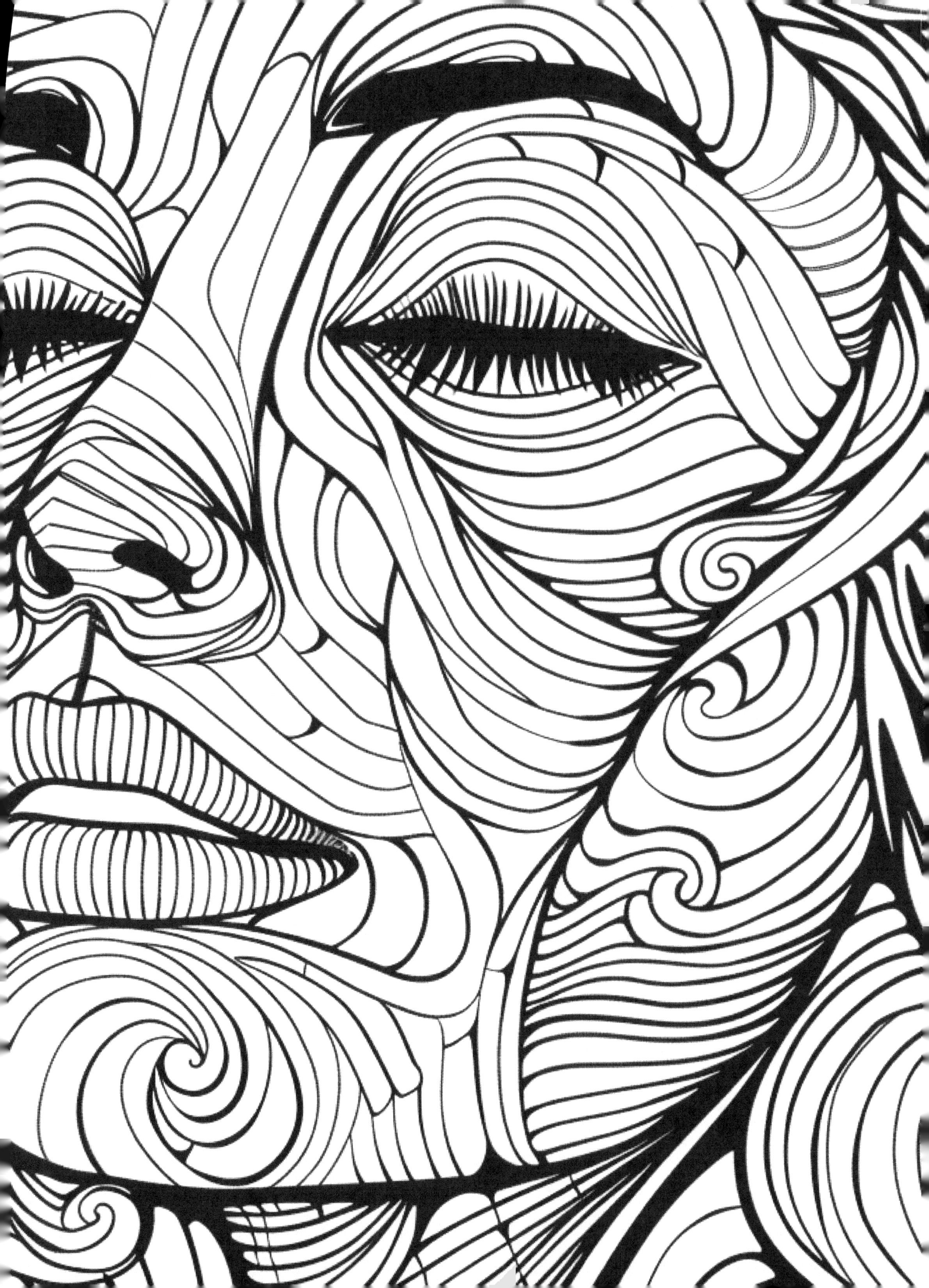

www.ingramcontent.com/pod-product-compliance
Lightning Source LLC
Chambersburg PA
CBHW062118220526
45471CB00010B/3791
9798320175331